MW01235911

I Met Another Dead Man Today

(and other stories from Printed Page Bookshop)

To ████████, IN APPRECIATION FOR YOUR FRIENDSHIP AND SUPPORT.

By Dan Danbom

I Met Another Dead Man Today
© 2023 by Dan Danbom

Better photos by Bob Keyser

Layout and Design by Andy Grachuk
www.JingotheCat.com

*To Barb Danbom and John Frantzen,
the best partners one could ever have.*

INTRODUCTION

by Fred Stoffel, a Denver Storyteller

The old time radio show "Escape" opened with:

> *"Tired of the everyday grind?*
> *Ever dream of a life of romantic adventure?*
> *Want to get away from it all?*
> *We offer you – ESCAPE!"*

I think of those lines because my friend Dan Danbom introduced me to the "theatre of the mind" – radio dramas from the '40s and '50s – years ago, and now I get to introduce him, his stories, and his store to you. But instead of Escape, think Printed Page Bookshop. It is a place for books, people, community, stories, a dog, and no shortage of romantic adventure. It is a time machine where the living come to learn from the dead. It is Denver's place of cool books and warm people. Printed Page is an unusual bookstore located in a beautiful small house on Denver's Antique Row on South Broadway. It's a cooperative store in which like-minded book sellers rent shelf space from the owners. At the same time, all the staff are familiar with and happily sell any book from any of the shelves. Against the odds of creating and succeeding as a small brick-and-mortar business, especially in our age of Amazon and eBooks, Printed Page has been open for 14 years. Dan and co-owner John Frantzen have survived lean financial times, endured the stress of a major reno-vation of Antique Row, and have outlasted the fear and constraints of Covid. "I Met Another Dead Man Today" is the captain's log of a grounded ark. There are tales of boundless curiosity, aimless wandering, senseless won-der, strange serendipity, unexpected revelation, meritless kindness, and astonishing grace.

Dan chronicles the comings and goings of customers and strangers at the little bookshop with winking glee and beguiling panache. Its snippets and vignettes capture the heart and marrow of Denver as customers traipse in with boxes of books and tales of toil and woe. The store's ethos is organic customer delight. The ambiance is of a com-fortable living room and modest country gathering place. Curious people buy books that, days before, were heaped up in piles, mounds, and boxes in the dusty and deso-late basements of the dead. Collectors tuck mementos of their lives between the pages of volumes that remain undisturbed and unknown until they are sorted, cleaned, and arranged for sale. Passages underlined by unknown savants cause one to wonder what struck another as so illuminating or important. The people thumbing through books become characters in feuilletons captured in a book clerk's imagination. A child given a used "Alice in Wonderland" discovered in the store will herself grow up to experience what it is to go down a modern rabbit hole. She may become a poet, an illustrator, or a gifted won-der like Mary Shelley. Books are the obvious essence of Printed Page. Books for and about people. Books sought after or stumbled upon. That is why the store has become a vital part of Denver and beyond. People come to the end of a trail on Antique Row in search of good tales. And their searches begin at the tail end of Dan's and the other dealers' quests to find the motherlodes of misplaced or underappreciated masterpieces.

I've seen Dan more crazed than the gold diggers in B. Traven's "Treasure of the Sierra Madre" when he's come across a pristine signed edition by one of the authors he's quietly sought out and stalked. The elation of the find is fleeting, and he's soon off seeking another satisfying fix.

As is often referenced in "I Met Another Dead Man Today," Dan and his wife, Barb, are deeply engaged in meeting unfortunate people and the homeless, acknowledging their hardships, and taking real actions to ameliorate the common woe. Their good works are a piece of the bookstore. There are real people before there are any stories.

Physical bookstores have always been spaces of timeless hope, curiosity, contemplation, erudition, ease, and wonder. There's an ineffable but tangible linkage to humanity that comes from holding a book in your hands. Particularly when the book has re-emerged from a shelf or nightstand or from beside a reading chair in some unknown reader's life. Or from forgotten tombs of tomes described in the pages of "I Met Another Dead Man Today." reclaimed and reshelved at Printed Page.

Some Days Are Better Than Others

AUGUST 17, 2018

A woman with a thick Russian accent came into Printed Page today. She asked for a book about Jimmy Carter and bought a book about uranium prospecting. I believe I have the beginnings of a conspiracy of some sort, but don't know what to do next. I'm going to ask for suggestions. I saved her credit card receipt and have her fingerprints on my glasses.

AUGUST 28, 2018

I drove to Castle Rock today to look at some books. The 80-ish woman selling them greeted me by telling me she had terminal cancer. Books always seem to come to me as a result of some big event: Someone's moving, someone's dying, someone's died.

I saw on her bookcase an award from Continental Airlines for having retired after 30 years, so I asked her about what it was like back in those days. She remembered how stewardesses (they weren't yet "flight attendants") had to weigh in before every flight, had supervisors stick them with pins to prove they were wearing girdles, had to answer questions about their last period. Remember the ads? *"I'm Cheryl. Fly me."* It seems so demeaning now, but at one time, being a stewardess was considered an exciting and desirable job. She managed to last 30 years in it. She enjoyed talking, and I got the sense there weren't a lot of people around she could talk to. I stayed too long, and then gave her a bit of more bad news: Her books were nearly worthless. It didn't seem to bother her a lot. And, this time, not finding any books after a long drive didn't bother me a lot either.

SEPTEMBER 11, 2018

This has been a slow few months for finding good books. Any bookseller who tells you that finding books isn't the fun part of this business is a liar. Speaking of liars, they'll call me up and say anything to get me to their house. These are the kind of people who used to try to talk you into going on a blind date, with descriptions like "good personality," "really nice," and "full set of teeth."

I'll ask them what kind of books they have, and they'll say "everything!" What genres? "Lots." How many books? "So many, they're all over the place. You really need to come out and look at these."

The less specific they are, the less likely I'm going to find any books I can use. Invariably, when I get to their house, the books bear no resemblance to how they were described. They must think that once I see books I'm not interested in, I'll be interested in them. Instead, they waste my time and theirs. My last house call involved a guy who said he's tried selling online to no avail (always a flashing red light). I could see that one problem he had in selling his books was that he didn't know what he wanted for them. I knew what I wanted: I wanted to go home.

SEPTEMBER 16, 2018

I remember a bookseller once telling me that this wasn't a business of scholars, it was one of mules. That lesson came home today when my partner and I again ventured out to Junk Cars in the Front Yard, Colorado, to go through several hundred boxes of books in a steel shipping container. It was 90+ degrees, and it reminded me of that scene in The Bridge on the River Kwai when the Japanese put a British officer in a metal box to torture him. He didn't have books to pass the time, or a lantern to give him some light. But then again, he didn't have to take down 50-pound boxes, open them, go through them, and then stack them back up. I came away exhausted and reeking of sweat and too many Mary Higgins Clark books, but I was rewarded by a lights-out first edition of *The Manchurian Candidate*. This was our sixth trip to the shipping container. Apparently, a cat got in on our last visit and had been locked in the container for a week. When we opened the door, it bolted like a cat out of hell. I think it was glad to see us.

SEPTEMBER 21, 2018

Some strange goings-on at Printed Page this week. A guy came in, asked to see some of our more valuable books, then took photos of them and left. We think he may be trying to sell the books to someone. If that someone bites, he'll come back in and buy the book so he can mark it up and deliver it to them.

I believe this idea of selling things you don't have was pioneered by Lehman Brothers, or maybe Enron. It's fine with me. Our visitor tries to get me to lower prices on books, so I think that lends credence to my theory.

"This book at $150 is outrageous," he said today. So I said, okay, let's look it up. The cheapest copy we could find online was $180, but it was in poor condition. One in better condition and comparable in other ways was $600. I told him I should probably re-price my book to at least $200. This information made him make a face like he'd stepped in something that came out of a sick Pekinese. Maybe next time he comes in, I'll ask him if I can take his picture. "Do the Pekinese face," I'll suggest.

September 24, 2018

Some books that I acquire need repair. I've always left that to the professionals. I don't send out a book worth $20, but if it's worth $200 or $1,000, it's worth it to me to invest the money and get the job done right. Still, I've been tugged in the direction of doing some simple repairs myself – fixing a torn page, or re-attaching a loose page, for example. I'm also a sucker for book-related stuff, so I bought some Neutral Ph Binding Adhesive and some Filmoplast Paper Mending Tape (as seen on TV!) and set to work practicing on some cheap books. Today, I finished my first project. I successfully glued a book to my work-bench. It's just a start. I know this stuff requires practice.

October 29, 2018

We volunteer at an apartment house for the homeless, the St. Francis Apartments. Some of the folks there have traumatic brain injuries, which is why they became homeless in the first place. A week or so ago, one was at a store in Arapahoe County, got confused, and ended up getting arrested. When he was released, he couldn't figure out how to get home, so he decided to sleep under a warm truck. Well, the truck later ran over his leg, and he ended up in Denver Health. Worse for him, the only reading material he could find was a Danielle Steel novel. Obviously, this is a guy who can't catch a break. His caseworker asked if we could find him some Stephen King, so we got him three books from Printed Page, or about 10 pounds worth. It's interesting to us what the people at the apartment take from the library we set up. Dictionaries are particularly popular. By the way, I think it's a misconception to think dictionaries are used mostly by less intelligent persons; in my experience, it's just the opposite.

Our friend will be laid up for another week or so. I have a feeling nothing he'll read in Stephen King will be as scary as what he lived on the street.

DECEMBER 5, 2018

One of the booksellers at Printed Page is in a rough patch. He's started showing signs of dementia and can't live independently any more.

Several years ago, another one of our booksellers, Pat Grego, had the same fate. John and I were determined to do everything we could to keep her engaged with books because we knew books were her life. So we compensated for her and helped her stay active in the store. Pat struggled for a few months before she died.

Anyway, we've approached our new situation the same way: Books are what our colleague lives for - they're what gives him a sense of purpose and accomplishment, and what's life without that? So yesterday, I picked him up at his assisted living facility and took him to the house of a guy who was selling his uncle's library. My friend was happy to get out and to book-scout again, and he was so proud that he found some nice things. He is as sharp as ever about books. When we were done, I asked him what he wanted for lunch. "Ice cream," he said. And ice cream it was.

When I got home and started going through the books I'd taken, I noticed that one had a distinctive identifying dealer code next to the price. It was Pat Grego's. It seemed like a fitting end to a good day.

FEBRUARY 13, 2019

Today was a day of lows and highs at Printed Page. A cold wind scoured the street - maybe that's why we didn't have any customers. Toward afternoon, an elderly couple came in wanting to sell some books. Had to downsize, they said. The books were in boxes roped together on a dolly with knots not seen outside a sailboat. The man carefully untied and unpacked them. The books were all common titles, well-worn mass market paperbacks: John Grisham, James Patterson, the kind of things that fill the shelves at Goodwills. I felt so sorry for them having made such an obvious exertion to no productive end. I found a Modern Library copy of *Out of Africa* and gave them as much as I could for it. And while I told them I couldn't speak for other book dealers, I said I didn't think they would have any better luck selling the other books. We loaded them back up, and off they went. It's saddening to have to tell people their books have little value.

As it was getting dark, a guy from Mississippi named Dustin came in. He wanted to know if the "Green Book" was real (it is). We talked for a while, and then he saw a book about juke joints. He got excited. "My daddy had a juke joint in Clay County Mississippi," he said, and started thumbing through the book. He turned a page, and there it was: the L&N, complete with the bright green walls, the pool table, and the wall light made from an Old Milwaukee beer can. "I gotta call my mama!" Dustin said, and he FaceTimed her. Mama knew the book and the photographer well. She said she had a copy once but lost it in a fire. She told Dustin the book  was hard to find and cost a lot. He laughed and said, "I don't want this man to know that!" But I did. It was $150.

He told her goodbye. Then he sat in a chair, staring at the pictures, tears running down his face, reminiscing about his father. "You know what?" I said. "I think you need this book more than I do. Take it."

He didn't think I was serious. "What? You don't mean it, right?"

"Take it."

"I'm gonna send it to my mama," he said.

"You do that. Tell her Happy Valentine's Day."

Some days are better than others.

MAY 7, 2019

We get to know a lot of people after it's too late to meet them. Their books tell me who they were. Go into a stranger's house and look at their books, and you'll come as close as possible to reading their mind. The other day, I got to meet Warren through the books his widow brought me.

She came in with her daughter and granddaughter, a little uncomfortable with her situation and unsure about what she was doing. With her white gloves and purse, she reminded me of my grandmother. Her daughter guided her to a chair, and then she and I went through the books.

Warren loved books, particularly books about books. I know he loved them because he cared for them so well, fashioning custom covers for them from book-themed wrapping paper. He took care to leave information in his books: where this one came from, what bindery rebound that one. He had a lot of copies of The Colophon, a richly produced hardbound periodical from the '30sthat cost more per issue than a lot of people made in a day back then.

I asked the daughter what she wanted for the books. She didn't know. So I made an offer and she took it. I wrote a check to the widow. She seemed happy that someone appreciated the books.

When I got the books home and did some more research, I concluded that the books were worth more than I paid for them. So I wrote another check – two, actually. I had made the first one out to Warren. What was I thinking?

JUNE 6, 2019

I got a call on Monday that has bothered me since. A woman I'd bought some books from angrily said, "I sold you some first editions. You gave me $3 apiece, and I want to know what you sold them for." I told her if I paid her $3, I would price the book at $9 or $10.

"Do you remember the titles?" I asked. She didn't. "I'd give you the books back if you tell me the titles." No dice. I asked. "You know that a lot of first editions aren't valuable, right?"

And she said, "I want you to know I'm on to you."

"What do you want me to do?".

"I just want you to know that I know what you did. Goodbye."

I looked up when I'd bought her books. It was ten months ago. Ten months she stewed about this, finally reaching some kind of point where she had to call. Ten months is a long time to carry around pent-up anger. I wondered what finally made her call.

Today was another house call. A woman was selling her parents' books. I asked her what she wanted. She didn't know, so I made her an offer, and after some back and forth we made a deal. When I got home, a $20 bill fell out of the first book I opened. I called her, told her about that, and suggested she check for cash in all the remaining books. If you hide money in one book, my experience is you will hide it in another. I put the $20 in the mail.

It would be weird if she waited ten months, then called to thank me.

JULY 3, 2019

The used/rare/antiquarian book business has a reputation for stuffiness, some deserved, some not. But I think it does itself no favors by booksellers increasingly using the word "curated." I started seeing this word a few years ago, now I see it all the time. "Our collection is carefully curated," is a frequent phrase in book circles. So I was gratified to see the word addressed in *Dryer's English: An Utterly Correct Guide to Clarity and Style.* "This is what 'curate' is good for: to serve as a noun identifying a junior clergyman...as a verb describing the work of a museum's staff organizing and presenting works of art.

"This is what 'curate' is not good for: to portray what you're doing when you're organizing a playlist of motivating songs for gym use, selecting smoked fishes for a brunch, or arranging displays of blouses, espadrilles, and picturesque thrift-shop books at Anthropologie."

There's a guy online who says his books are "hand-selected." He'd be ripe for "curate" use, particularly if he calls his store an "emporium" or "gallery," or has "Ltd." after its name. And now it's not just that your stock is "curated," it is "carefully curated." It strikes me as an affectation, and it probably says to customers that the books are going to be more expensive.

Anyway, my books are not curated. If I see a book I like and I think I can sell it, I put it on my shelf. And no, I don't "hand select" it. I use special bibliographic tongs.

July 24, 2019

I don't know what it is about this summer, but the past few days at Printed Page have had more people coming in wanting to sell books than buy them. Bookselling professionals have a word for this: bankruptcy.

Yesterday brought an antique dealer whose books had nothing to distinguish them except their age. He was followed by a woman who thought it wise to rid all her books of their dust jackets. Then there was a widow wanting to sell her husband's books. She came in with her daughter and left happy to have some money. Most of the books we're offered are just random accumulations. There are few true collections, but today brought one of those.

A woman brought in a collection of Nancy Drew books in condition rarely seen. She had done her homework and had bibliographic information on every volume. She'd also done her homework on me, and was thorough enough to have uncovered my arrest as a teenager for Interstate Flight To Avoid Vegetables. I've never had anyone do that before, but she'd had a career in a field where prudence was valued.

Collections like this one don't come along often. This one even included the rare *Nancy's Mysterious Growth* and *Nancy's Secret Chiropodist.*

AUGUST 5, 2019

I met another dead man today. His name was Gordon. He liked Harleys and original abstract art, made his own ammunition and bought expensive books he never read (though he took the time to paste bookplates in most of them).

It's a game I play to try to figure out what someone was like by what they left behind. I don't know what he did for a living, but it made him money. He built a fancy home in a marginal part of town. He had a three-car garage. The front faced a busy avenue. The back was on a private lake I never knew existed.

His daughter was unusually unemotional about dealing with his estate. I tried to make conversation as I looked through the books. My questions about him were answered in a word or two, no more. She volunteered nothing.

He had a few books about wine that suggested an interest, and a wine cellar that suggested a lot more than that. When I went to find her after finishing with the books, she was in a large kitchen with hundreds of bottles of wine lined up on the counters. "How do you sell those?" I asked, and she told me her caterer would buy them.

As I left, I told her I had lost my father too, and I knew what she was going through. She shrugged. "It's okay," she said, and I left, wondering what my heirs will say about me when I'm gone. At least they won't have to worry about my leaving that much wine. Never touch the stuff.

August 7, 2019

Let me just start by saying that it's as impossible for a bookseller to evaluate a book based on a photo as it is for a doctor to tell you about your health based on the photo of a urine sample (I learned my lesson *that* time!). So when a guy sent me a photo of a Harry Potter book today and asked what it was worth, while also saying it was going for $5000 online, I suggested to him that he should sell his book to the person who thinks it is worth $5000. He angrily responded that I should learn how to read. He did not want advice. He wanted to know what it was worth. So see if you can guess how I responded:

1) I inquired if he had a lot of success insulting persons from whom he sought free advice.

2) I told him his book was worth $10,000, told him I knew of someone who would pay cash for it, and gave him the name of a friend at another book store as a prank.

3) I said I would be happy to appraise his book and gave him my hourly rate (valued at $1000 per hour on eBay).

4) I told him his email account had been hacked by someone whose parents were brother and sister.

5) I ignored him.

One of those responses is true. You go ahead and guess.

August 11, 2019

We haven't seen Buddy in several weeks at Printed Page Bookshop. Buddy used to come in late in the day, pick a book about magic off the shelf, and read it for a half-hour or so. Sometimes he'd ask to change clothes in our bathroom. He was often sunburned, which living on the street will do to you.

Buddy's not the first homeless person who has found refuge in the store. Others have welcomed getting inside from the elements, being offered a drink of water, and left alone to sit and read. One living behind the store liked our leftover pizza. Another used our tools to fix his bike.

I think the most important thing I've learned is not to judge these folks. One of the residents at the St. Francis Center told me that when she was on the street, people would step over her to help a dog. She said that with tears in her eyes. She, like all the others at St. Francis, have their own stories to tell. I haven't heard a happy one yet. This week our friend is being tested for brain injury at a Denver hospital. She's asked for us to send good vibes her way.

I hope Buddy's doing well. Yesterday someone bought his magic book. Now I wish I'd saved it for him. If he comes back, we'll just have to find another.

AUGUST 31, 2019

We feel Denver's population boom at Printed Page. Today we had customers from Massachusetts, Alabama, New York, California, and Kansas, all new to the city.

We also had a customer visiting from Missouri. He is what we call a "Discreet Purchaser." He would rather his wife – who accompanied him – not know that he is buying books in a certain price range. He will hand me such books with a wink, and I put them under the counter. And then he will say, a little too loudly, "Well, I guess I don't see anything I need today. Let's go, Honey." I go along with this. I'm not going to cause any marital discord unless the purchase is under $50. Instead, I will ship him the books in a plain brown box with the return address of Printed Page Auto Parts, or New Vistas Elevator Shoe Company, or Little Moo Home Veal Raising Kit.

Anyway, for some persons, finding a new used bookstore in their new city is right up there with finding a new dentist or doctor. I think a dentist would be smart to hang out here and let people know that they need to invest in their smiles. It would be okay with me unless he started giving people the stink-eye when they opened our jar of candy.

Toward the end of the day, some locals finally came in – a group of about six teenage girls. They parked themselves in the back room and talked and laughed for an hour or so. That was fine with me, too.

SEPTEMBER 20, 2019

Golf's never made me feel good – "klutzy" is more the word – but that isn't true for everyone. One of our friends from the St. Francis Apartments used to play a lot before his brain injury. Now he doesn't get much of a chance, but it makes him feel better when he does. He has lost a lot, but not his love for golf.

So he and I and one of the staff went out to play yesterday. It was a beautiful day, and we had fun. I hadn't played in so long, I'd forgotten all my bad habits.

We sat at a picnic table and talked afterward. When he was homeless, he spent a lot of time at the Denver Public Library. Because of his brain injury, he needed the quiet of the library – and the roof over his head. He told us that friends who used to work at a golf course would let him in at night and he'd camp there. He was safe from other people, but the coyotes gave him a hard time. He fought them off with a strobe light from his bicycle and a golf club he found at Goodwill.

One day at the library, a social worker approached him. She connected him with various services for veterans and people with injuries like his. He hit the jackpot when he got to move into the St. Francis Apartments, where we met him.

I learned, too, that he liked to cook. As luck would have it, I had some cookbooks in my car, so I passed those along to him.

All in all, it was the best day I've had at golf in a long time.

I Met Another
Dead Man Today

NOVEMBER 15, 2019

Lyman Rhoades was one of the booksellers at Printed Page. He was a lawyer who found a love of bookselling late in life, and often wished aloud that he had found it earlier. He would come into the store in the afternoon, plant himself in an easy chair, and hold court. He could talk to anyone about anything, and he did. He knew as much about books as anyone I've ever known.

Lyman cared deeply about the poor and society's underdogs, and he was generous with them with his money, time, and talent. He went with me once to deliver food for the food bank, and I could tell it affected him deeply to see people in such need. Lyman died earlier this year.

Yesterday, his family gave us most of his clothes to give to the folks at the St. Francis Center. When people die, their books get dispersed to the four winds. Same with their possessions, and their clothes. But this time, it'll be different. Now when I'm down at St. Francis, I'll see someone in Lyman's favorite down vest, or in one of his signature turtlenecks. And I'll think of him. Maybe remember the time when he launched into a discourse about the true first edition of *The Catcher in the Rye*, or the time he gave his Broncos season tickets away then had to sue the guy he gave them to regain the rights to buy the playoff tickets. (He won the suit, then turned around and gave the guy the tickets. It was a matter of principle, you see.)

It'll be nice to be reminded of Lyman, and I think he would have approved that the underdogs and the poor are now wearing the shirts off his back.

DECEMBER 10, 2019

A man came into the store yesterday with great fanfare. He was the kind of guy you'd expect to see wearing a wool cape and using terms like "my good man."

"Let me see your finest first editions!" he asked, and I showed him copies of *Ulysses, Atlas Shrugged, A Child's Christmas in Wales*, and a bunch of others. He carefully looked through each one and noted his approval of the prices. He even made a decent stack of them on the counter. At one point, we had a lengthy discussion about the demise of brick-and-mortar stores like Printed Page. He thought that was a sad development, and wondered aloud why that was. Eventually he settled on a $10 copy of *Soul on Ice*. He offered $5 for it. He left empty-handed, but at least now we don't have to wonder why brick-and-mortar stores are disappearing.

DECEMBER 28, 2019

I don't think I've spent a better day as a bookseller than the day I had today at Printed Page. A friend I worked with several careers ago brought his granddaughter in. It's her dream to own a bookstore, so she wanted to know what it was like. I told her about my experience, but my thoughts kept going back to that scene in The Graduate where the guy advised Dustin Hoffman: "Plastics." Her grandparents bought her a book, and I gave her a copy of *Slightly Chipped*, a memoir of the book business I thought she might enjoy.

A group from Tennessee came in, and the patriarch said, "Do you know who our only illiterate President was? He came from Tennessee." Well, yes, I do know, because I am a professional bookseller for crying out loud: Andrew Johnson. The Tennessean cleaned out our Andrew Johnson section and walked out with both books.

A woman came in and said, "Where is Stephen King?"

I answered, "Maine."

She didn't buy anything.

Later a guy came in and we got to talking about the symbolism of books. I told him of a customer who once ordered 160 feet of books just to decorate his house. The customer said he was a filmmaker and was once in a Hollywood mansion that was a set for a movie. It had a fantastic library, except that all the books were, in reality, just painted on a wall. It fooled him. I thought it would be cheaper just to buy the books, but – full disclosure – I don't own a mansion.

We have some props in our shop. My fiction section has a typewriter. My partner's mystery section features a pair of handcuffs. A young woman brought them to the counter and wanted to buy them. The sight of a young woman approaching me with handcuffs "triggered" me, so I told her the handcuffs were not for sale, as I silently calculated whether I could outrun her.

JANUARY 3, 2020

Another day at Printed Page, another crowd of interesting people. They wanted to talk about Upton Sinclair, Isaac Newton, and Franz Kafka. We had a group of scientists come in from Boulder who liked witchcraft and vintage science fiction. Another group was talking about the most frightening book they had ever read. One said *The Exorcist*. Another said *In Cold Blood*.One asked me for my vote. I said my choice was a book so frightening that we will never, ever stock it in Printed Page: *Introduction To Calculus*. I still have nightmares.

One guy came in. He was missing the middle finger on his right hand. As he signed the credit card receipt, I asked him how he lost the finger. He said it was amputated as part of a plea bargain when he was charged with road-rage.

No wonder so many people ask if we have any job openings.

I get satisfaction from selling books. I get pleasure from finding them. Every bookseller I know likes to talk about their finds. Finding books animates them. Selling them? Meh.

I got a call the other day from a professional organizer. She wanted me to meet her at a house to buy books from one of her hoarder clients. "This woman has a sickness," the organizer told me, and my house call would presumably aid in her recovery.

As I looked at the books, the organizer shielded the woman from seeing what I was doing. When I was done, I wrote out a check and started to carry the books out to my car. The woman started crying, almost shrieking. She pleaded with me to leave this book, then that one. I let her take back what she wanted as the organizer gave me a dirty look. The woman followed me out as I loaded the books. "Please, could I keep this book? This one?" I told her to take them. I felt as if I were complicit in some kind of cruel scheme to separate someone from what they loved.

It was a reminder to me of how much books mean to people, almost as if they are members of the family. And it was a reminder to respect that, and to do my best never to be in that situation again.

FEBRUARY 13, 2020

Today was a strange one at Printed Page. A couple came in and said they had been searching for years for *Sunset Slope* by Wilson Rockwell, a fairly obscure guy who wrote about Western Colorado. As luck would have it, we had a sweet first edition in a dust jacket for just $20. The couple was delighted. They took turns looking at it, reading passages aloud, and telling me again and again how happy they were to have found it.

Then they handed me the book, said "goodbye," and left.

Next into the store was a guy who showed me a picture on his phone. "This book was here the last time I was in, and I came back to buy it." It was a copy of Tolkien's *Tree*. No, I told him, it sold last month. He found some other books. He wanted them all, but passed on two.

I said, "You know what happens when you don't buy a book you want, don't you?" I told him I'd hold the books for him for a week. But there is a lesson here: If you are ever in a bookstore –or, at least, in *my* bookstore - and you see a book you even remotely think you want, you should buy it immediately without second thought, or face the very real possibility that the rest of your life will be lived in regret and self-loathing.

FEBRUARY 18, 2020

Like any business, the used book business can be tough. We worry about the health of Printed Page, how we can do better by our customers, how we're going to pay for a new swamp cooler or handle that new property tax bill that reminds us we live in an increasingly expensive city.

Then comes along a day like Saturday, when everything good and satisfying about what we do manifests itself in the course of a few hours.

We had people who traveled miles to see us, and others who just came in on a whim...casual readers and serious collectors...people eager to pile up books on the counter to buy, others eager to pile up books on the counter to sell...home-schooled kids who came in with their teacher...a nurse exhausted and demoralized by a work environment that asks more for less...a young couple who parked themselves in a nook, bought nothing, then returned later to linger again, as if the simple act of being around books gave them some sort of sustenance...a regular who comes in mostly to listen to our music, take photographs, and offer our shop dog, Izzy, treats...a long-time customer whose wife died after a lengthy illness, now trying his best to climb out of the pit of his grief and wanting only friendship and conversation.

Late in the day, a woman brought in a collection of catalogs from a California bookseller. Turns out she and the bookseller once worked for Jake Zeitlin.

I said, "I know who Jake Zeitlin was."

"Zate-lin," she corrected, "and he would have let you know that, too."

I promised to send her some materials I had from him. I sometimes think most of what I know about books was passed on to me by others, and some of what others know I passed on myself.

The day ended profitably in pretty much every way I could think of. When I got home, I saw that the nurse had left a review for us on Google: "Like a little ray of sunshine in a foggy forest. Just lovely."

And even more profitable than I thought.

March 3, 2020

I met another dead man today. His widow, Donna, introduced me to him. She said he had died recently and, to use her words, his death was brutal. She called to see if I would come out to her house to look at his thousands of books.

I find these situations so hard. On the one hand, it's exciting to think of buying a new library. On the other, how can you get excited by the byproduct of someone's death? What is the fun of going into a house furnished in grief?

So we didn't talk about books. We talked about Arthur. He was a printer, a postal worker, a cabbie. He was a handy guy who could fix anything. He got his love of reading from his teacher parents. He had a great sense of humor. I told Donna I wish I'd have known him. She said I would have liked him.

I'll go out to Donna's house next week. Maybe I can help her with the books. And maybe I can get to know Arthur better.

April 21, 2020

[Denver is in the middle of a stay-at-home order because of the Coronavirus pandemic. Printed Page has been closed for several weeks]

If a prestigious marketing program at a university ever invites me to lecture and a student asks, "Sir? What do you do in your book store to get customers to come in?" I would answer, "I start eating lunch or urgently need to go to the bathroom." These options have shown over the course of many years to make that front door open with customers who have lots of questions demanding my uninterrupted attention.

But what do you do when you can't have your door open because of a stay-at-home order? At Printed Page, we've embarked on a special effort to make sure that when we are finally able to open the door, awe-struck customers will exclaim, "I've never seen such neat shelving!"

Crowd-pleasing shelving starts with a visual inspection from a trained looker. Shelves with books that aren't uniformly straight are flagged for further action. Using a manual level, the shelving technician makes an initial assessment of both vertical and horizontal uniformity to determine what is known in the trade as perpendicularity. After lunch, another technician uses laser technology to assess and determine a straight line on which the volumes will stand. The laser level guides the technician to either move a volume forward or backward. Quality control inspectors check the work for, well, quality control. At that point the shelf is certified as meeting the requirements of the International Protocols on Shelving Books and is ready for public viewing.

We intend to let all the Neat Shelving clubs around the country know of our achievement in the hope that we'll be a stop on one of their national bus tours. These clubs have names like "Shelfless Vagabonds" and "Board Housewives." Many are shelving re-creators who show off their skills in national shelving competitions. Those who participate in the book divisions strive to be able to remove a book from a shelf in such a way as to not leave an unsightly gap. Here's where years of practice really pay off.

AUGUST 22, 2020

A steady stream of customers flowed through Printed Page today, starting with a woman from Joes, Colorado, looking for something for her son and ending with a guy from Tennessee, inspired by his trip West to look for books by Edward Abbey. In between was a young FBI agent who saves up to add to her collection of fine bindings, a guy who bought every movie book we had that referenced sleaze creatures – I took a chance and mentioned to him that Steve Bannon was in Chapter 6 – and seekers of Edith Wharton, Stephen King, T.S. Eliot, Jack London, Aldous Huxley, Mary Shelley, Rudyard Kipling, Haruki Murakami, Tolstoy, and Tolkien.

A woman who had just moved here from San Diego told me how happy she was to find us in her neighborhood. I asked her if she had registered to vote yet. She hadn't, so I had her register right then and there. Full service book store.

One couple told me they were looking for a certain title that I thought I heard to be *Killers of the Flower Moon*. When I presented it to them, they said no, they wanted *Empire of the Summer Moon*. "Work with me!" I implored, but they wouldn't.

Toward the end of the day, the Tennessean came in. He bought *Desert Solitaire, War and Peace, Lincoln in the Bardo,* and, I'll be damned, he found a copy somewhere of *Empire of the Summer Moon*.

Sometimes, it just happens that way.

SEPTEMBER 9, 2020

The first customer in today was a Holocaust denier. She was looking for David Irving's books. She said she liked him because he "wanted to get to the bottom" of the Holocaust and could because he can read German. "What do you think about that?" she asked me.

"What do I think of the Holocaust? Well, my dad was among the troops that liberated Dachau. I know he didn't think it was made up."

SEPTEMBER 19, 2020

Today brought the following persons into Printed Page immediately after I began eating my lunch:

A woman with seven children who quite appropriately collects different editions of Snow White and the Seven Dwarfs. Daughter Number four, who did not appear to be a dwarf, collects editions of *Alice in Wonderland.*

An Australian who collects Nancy Drew books and was surprised to learn that author Carolyn Keene was really a number of different women (which hasn't stopped at least one forger from signing "Carolyn Keene" in a Drew book).

A couple, looking for a baby gift, who bought a signed copy of *Charlotte's Web* that I would never let a baby get within ten feet of.

Paul, our taciturn plumber, who fixed a leak in the swamp cooler. Ever since he told me he was on an underwater demolition team in the Navy, I have never quibbled with him about his bill.

An FBI agent and her roommate. She is on a Sebastian Faulks kick.

A British woman from Stratford-upon-Avon looking for – no surprise – Shakespeare. Any customer with a British accent always buys books.

A young couple interested in European history and high-brow literature. She was in yesterday and brought him in today.

Another repeat customer from yesterday brought his wife in to show her around. I was glad I remembered his name. He was an orphan from the Korean War adopted by a Denver Minister 65 years ago. People who bring in their friends go right to the top of my "Most Favored Persons" list.

And a chess player who bought three of our chess books. He had them in his bag before I could ring them up, as he had thought two moves ahead.

OCTOBER 12, 2020

A couple of weeks ago, a guy came into Printed Page and asked us to tell him what a book was worth "because I don't want to have to pay to find out." The book was about a massacre of Native Americans near Loveland, Colorado. I am as sure that this didn't happen as I am sure that Columbus didn't discover Las Vegas. We gave him some ideas on where he could find out for himself and sent him on his way.

On Friday, he came back. This time, he wanted to trade worthless books for worthy ones.

He started asking about our stock. "Do you have any books on Mormons?" Why, yes, here are some. "Do you have any books on 18th century American history?" Right here. "How about CS Lewis?" Yes. "Anything on early astronomy?" Yes..

He talked the entire time he was browsing, which is okay. He asked my opinion of Papal indulgences, Denver's growth, public education, and whether I believed in lawn aeration. On and on and on for two hours.

Not surprisingly, he left without buying anything. He asked me to hold a book for him to pick up later in the day. I think he was testing us. I imagined him doing the same in Home Depot. "Got any Makita drills? How about refrigerators? Any carpet squares? Thank you. See you later."

He never came back for the book. I was kind of thankful.

OCTOBER 24, 2020

Saturday was more interesting than normal at Printed Page. Morning was slow, so I was reduced to playing my "Which store will they enter?" game, where I try to guess where people passing by will go. If they get out of matte black cars, they will go to the tattoo place. If they are walking a dog, they will go to the pet food store. If they have glasses, there's a chance they'll come into Printed Page.

One couple from Aspen called in advance and were excited about some books we have. They spent two hours in the store ogling books, then left empty-handed. A young Latina from San Antonio strolled around the store and spent five minutes picking out $300 in books.

Then Ron came in. Ron is new to us, but visits often. His second trip in, he brought his wife who said she needed to come "to see what all the hullabaloo is about." Ron is

an orphan from the Korean War, abandoned by the Kore-
ans because his father was a Black serviceman. He grew up
in Denver in a pastor's family. He told me Saturday that he
learned we both once worked for the same company. He
said he was hired in the 70s because of his athletic ability
– that was a big deal back when companies valued brag-
ging rights. Ron was a meter reader in Denver's northwest
suburbs and was constantly approached by police who
asked what he was doing in their neighborhood. He spent
a lot of time in the backseat of police cars. Eventually, he
had to be transferred to a safer location. Now he works
with ex-cons. And he reads a lot of high-quality literature
and theology. He is a quiet, unassuming guy who exudes
decency, and we are honored to have him as a customer
– and as a reminder that, despite my passersby guessing
game, you can't judge people by how they look.

October 28, 2020

I met another dead man today. His widow had me
come to her house and go to their basement, where he
kept his books. He had died some time ago. I had the
feeling his wife regarded the area as sacrosanct and never
ventured there. It had the look of neglect and the smell of
a tomb.

The man who lived there had wide-ranging interests:
architecture, history, Western Americana, snakes – and a
lover.

I learned the last part when I was looking for a map
in an envelope attached to the back cover of a book, but
instead of having a map, it had a series of handwritten

notes that traced the passion that started the affair and the guilt that ended it.

Curiosity is essential to booksellers. You need it to fully understand a book's significance, whether it's a first edition, why it is or isn't important, whether a former owner was someone of historical importance.... In my experience, curiosity isn't something you can turn on and turn off. You either have it, or you don't. But it's not always rewarding.

I read the letters. I felt as if I was violating something, learning about these two people in a way they never wanted to be known. Yet they had left this record, and I had found it. I kept thinking of the woman upstairs.

When I was done looking at the books, I went back to write her a check. She told me her husband would be happy to know the books were going to someone who would appreciate them. She talked about his life, his accomplishments, and how much she missed him. Her voice broke as she spoke.

I don't know if she knew about the affair. But I do know she will never see those letters and never feel the new pain they would surely bring.

Aliens Created Us To Find Them Gold

November 26, 2020 — Thanksgiving

I was talking to some friends when one asked me if the homelessness situation in Denver had affected Printed Page. It has. We've had people camp in the alley behind the store – one was a woman afraid of shelters, another was a guy who told me he was using a handful of gravel to call home. We've given them food and water. A homeless guy named Buddy used to visit once in a while to use our bathroom and change his clothes. He'd always find a book he wanted and ask us to hold it for him. He never bought anything. We ended up making a gift of one book he particularly wanted.

I thought maybe Buddy had returned last week when a guy wrapped in a blanket came in and made a beeline for our wing chair, but it was someone else. John told me the man had been in the day before as well. He wasn't wearing a mask, so John gave him one. The next time he came in, he refused a mask and said his blanket was his mask. And he came in again and again, spending all day, every day. Earlier this week, he resisted a request to leave from one of the women staffing the store. Customers were avoiding the area where he had planted himself. So John stepped up yesterday to take a shift. Again, the homeless guy appeared, but John met him at the door and told him he had worn out his welcome. The expression is that the quality mercy is not strained, but sometimes, it is.

Now I know what public libraries go through.

There has to be a better answer. As we all consider our blessings today, that's what I'll be thinking about.

December 1, 2020

I'd never heard of William Henry Ireland until I started reading the autobiography of ASW Rosenbach, who was a colossus in the rare book world a century ago. He regarded Ireland as the greatest forger ever. At the age of 17, Ireland fooled almost the entire literary world with his "discovery" of many Shakespearean manuscripts. He expertly created all sorts of Elizabethan letters and poems, as well as a believable back story explaining how he had acquired them. He even wrote a pretended play of Shakespeare's. That proved to be his undoing, but not the end of him. He became such a folk hero that "there suddenly sprang up a great demand to behold the handiwork of this delectable young villain." People in England, and curio collectors everywhere, wanted to own specimens of his fraudulent papers, creating such a demand that he was kept busy from dawn to dark making forgeries of his forgeries. Another forger got tripped up when he did a forged account of the Battle of Hastings carelessly dated before the battle took place.

This timing stuff throws forgers off. I had a photograph of Humphrey Bogart in Printed Page signed in a felt tipped pen. Bogart died before the invention of felt-tipped pens. Although it wasn't for sale, a guy offered me so much for it that I had to let it go, even though it was a great conversation piece. I also had a woman offer me a copy of the "Warren Commission Report on the Assassination of President Kennedy" signed by President Kennedy. I should have commissioned her to make some more.

January 6, 2021

I met another dead man today. His name was Jerry. He was a Ph.D. who taught at a local university.

His house looked as if it had been abandoned a long time ago. Water from a leaking roof stained the walls and loosened the plaster. Rodents had lived there uncontested, spreading their waste high and low. Yet there was still food in the cabinets and clothes in the closets. Someone had also lived in a basement apartment. It would not have surprised me to find a body there.

For whatever reason, Jerry was well-armed. Dresser drawers overflowed with ammunition, and aged boxes of cartridges were strewn around the floors.

I came away thinking that maybe Jerry saw threats from the outside world that blinded him to the greater threat he posed to himself: living alone, no one to care for him, not being bothered with the vestiges of civilized living.

I looked indifferently at the books I could get to. It wasn't exactly the kind of place that invited one to linger, but neither was it the kind of place I will easily forget.

JANUARY 19, 2021

Today at Printed Page was one for the accidental tourists. Not a single visitor today planned to come in. One was just walking by, one was waiting for a friend to get her hair cut, another was waiting for her own tattoo.

The one waiting for a tattoo is an ICU nurse in Loveland. She said that, after the Thanksgiving Covid rush, things slowed down a bit, but now her hospital is taking patients who are being flown in from North and South Dakota. She seemed to take it all in stride. I suppose otherwise you couldn't be a nurse.

As it got near closing time, a guy surveyed the store and proclaimed, "I don't have time to read." I've heard this a lot, usually delivered with the implication that only we slackers have time to read while others are in the big, important work that makes our decadent lives possible. I've never understood why someone would say this. How do they get information? How do they learn? How do they expand their minds? How do they carry on a conversation? If you "don't have time to read," you better make some. You're doing something wrong. He didn't buy anything. That's wrong, too.

Even though we've had Printed Page for more than 11 years, every day is different. Today started with my first visit from a customer via FaceTime: A young woman was a new mom, and a friend wanted to get her some books, so I virtually showed the mom around the store while she held her baby, Iris. All Iris's sisters are named after flowers, I learned: Rose and Violet. (Breaking the mold, Iris's brother is named after jeans: Levi.) It worked out pretty well. Mom picked up a small stack of books, and Iris was the first beneficiary of our Baby Gets A Free Book policy.

Shop dog Izzy picked up the patterns of the store quickly, waiting until a customer came in to demand to be let out in back to pee. "You're in charge," I said to the

customer as I took Izzy out. When we came back in two minutes later, she'd increased sales by 63%.

A couple of friends came in, one to get a book a grown child regretted not keeping from childhood, the other to share stories about mutual friends in Denver journalism circles and generally just to talk, which we did most successfully. While he was in, a street person was picnicking on the sidewalk in front, and having a lively conversation too, although with himself. When I went out front later, I saw that he'd left a lot of food, most of it curiously still in packages.

A friend I hadn't seen in 20 years came by, too. I told him he hadn't aged a bit, and he lied that I hadn't, either.

Later in the day, a customer and I got to talking about autographed books. He asked about an autographed Ayn Rand book we'd had. I told him it had sold, but I had seen that someone had put up Ayn Rand's ashtray for sale for only $250. Not signed, just stained.

FEBRUARY 21, 2021

Yesterday was a welcome relief from the monotony of Covid life. First I got my second shot, and second, I worked my first Saturday at Printed Page in a long time.

From the moment we opened, a steady stream of people poured through the store. A couple with a new baby came in. We have baby books we give to new parents. Baby Luca got a book on dinosaurs. I told his parents that when he could read it in a couple of months, he should come in and read it to me (not that I couldn't read it myself just in case you're wondering).

A British expatriate bought our celebrated *History of Cannibalism* after I pointed out to her that it has a recipe for Manwiches. Her companion gave me a long list of books he wanted. When I presented him with one, he confessed that he had just bought it from another store. I told him to get the hell out.

A man and his daughter came in. It turns out we have a mutual friend who's established a prize for young bibliophiles. Upon hearing this, she became its first entrant.

Some people linger in the store for an hour or so, sometimes buying something, sometimes not, but I admire their approach more than the guy who breezes in, finds something, and leaves within a couple of minutes. Saturday was linger-intensive.

Around 2:00, I started to get over-heated and thought I was having side effects from the shot until I had a flash of panic, thinking I might violate the retail principle of never passing out on the sales floor without a supervisor's permission. But the feeling passed.

A young man right out of Georgetown graduate school came in. He wants to become one of our booksellers. That raises a whole bunch of questions, but in the meantime, he bought our first edition of *Ulysses,*which we have had past its best-by date.

By 3:00, I managed to wolf down my lunch, standing distant from everyone else and masking between bites.

At the end of the day, our friend Dave was in. Dave swore off drinking a couple of years ago and took up collecting books. He had eyed a couple of John Dunning's books earlier in the week and was ready to buy. Another customer beat him to the punch two hours earlier. I can't count the number of times this has happened, but, to reiterate, I really could read that dinosaur book if it came down to it.

MARCH 8, 2021

I met another dead man today. He was a Stanford graduate who commanded a B-24 squadron over Italy during WWII. He had survived being shot at and shot down. On a basement wall were framed aerial photos showing some of the targets he bombed. He later made a lot of money with his degree in Petroleum Engineering, and he lived in a mansion on one of the finest streets in one of Denver's finest neighborhoods. His wife, 97, had to move out of the house recently because it was just too big for her. She will do better in a single story place because she is scheduled for knee-replacement surgery.

The house had lots of books: leather-bound series of Hugo and Hawthorne, Emerson and Thoreau. There was a gorgeous set of books on French history – in French, *mon ami*. And there was lots of popular literature, and those Stanford textbooks that I suspect hadn't been touched in 70 years.

Part of the house had been converted into a kind of studio for the dead man's son. He's a motivational speaker who does something about performance warriors. He has a book out, and lots of copies were scattered around. We shared some stories about growing up in that part of Denver. I lived about two miles and $10 million from his house.

I left the house without buying a single book. Sometimes things work out that way. I guess I just wasn't motivated.

MARCH 11, 2021

There are all kinds of book people, and it seemed today that all of them came into Printed Page. First was a collector from Kansas City, who comes to Denver to see extended family, and comes to Printed Page to get away from them. He had eyed a first edition Steinbeck for months and today bought it with $100 bills. He explained that his book budget was funded by a part-time job he has cleaning parking lots. Maybe I'm in the wrong business.

While he was in, a young man came in asking if we had expensive books. He had been at the Broadmoor and had seen that they had books for sale for thousands of dollars, and he thought it might be fun for him to acquire some books like that. I told him my advice was to not just randomly buy books, but to have some focus and buy books you like. However, should he choose to ignore my advice and randomly spend large amounts of money, we would be glad to open the store early for him.

A woman from Chicago was distraught after reading a book about a horrific fire in an elementary school. She was desperate for something light to get her mind off it.

While I was helping her, another woman called. "Can you tell me if a book I have is valuable?" she asked.

"Yes," I said.

A customer from Durango came in. We hadn't seen Tom in a year or two. He used to come into our store when his wife was in a Denver hospital. He'd be here for weeks living out of a motel. We used to invite him for dinner, but, no, he wanted to be near the hospital. He told me she died in December. Now he was in town to go to a hospital for some tests.

I dished out some disappointment today. A woman who had some Seuss books on eBay – she said the bidding was up to hundreds of dollars on them before eBay suspended Seuss sales – brought the books in to sell them to me. She had advertised the books as first editions. I took no pleasure in showing her they weren't.

I think I disappointed another customer. He said he had put some books on hold. "What books were they?" I asked.

"I don't know," he answered.

"What name would the books be under?" I asked.

"I don't know," he answered.

I was unable to help him. He made me think that, like some other places, maybe we should start taking people's temperatures.

One book I was holding for a customer was Roald Dahl's *My Uncle Oswald*. He'd been looking for it for a long time, and we located a copy for him. He called to say he was a half-hour away and wanted to be sure I didn't close before he could make it in. I told him I'd wait. He was excited to get the book, handling it carefully and admiringly. It's a $20 book. I bet he gets more satisfaction from it than the guy who wants the $2000 books.

MARCH 30, 2021

I met another dead man today. He worked at a newspaper in the days when book publishers sent lots of books to newspapers, and he managed to acquire a lot. He was interested in computers, making money, home improvement, and finding love.

Through him, I met another dead person: his mother. Helen was an accomplished academic, a world traveler, and a person of faith. Among the books was a package of her papers: letters, report cards, diplomas, passports – the documentation of a life fully lived. There was also a return address on the box the papers were mailed in. I've written a letter to the sender explaining how I came to have these papers and asking if I could send them back. We'll see how that goes.

[Several weeks later, she responded that she would like to have the papers, so we sent them to her.]

APRIL 1, 2021

Some days are better than others at Printed Page.

Our first customer today was a woman who said she just decided she needed to buy a book today. She did.

It kind of went downhill from there. A guy wanted William Gibson's *Neuromancer*. We have lots of Gibson titles, but not that. He then asked for Asimov books. We have some Asimov, but not the ones he wants. The next woman wanted a copy of *84 Charing Cross Road*. We have one. It wasn't the one she wanted. A customer called for books by John Calvin. We have some Calvin and Hobbes, but no, not good enough. I wanted to scream, "You have to WORK WITH ME, people!"

To pour salt in the wound, a woman came in and asked directions to a competitor's store. I pointed her toward the rude and more expensive part of the neighborhood.

Around closing time, a guy rode up on a skateboard. When he came in, I remembered him: It was Buddy. Buddy is the homeless guy who would come in to change his shirt, have some water, and read. Last year, he coveted a magic book we had, but it sold. We found another and made sure he got it for Christmas.

He came in to thank me. He said he had been in and out of jail, but finally "hit my number" – made parole – and was now working at a screen printing place. He said he rarely came to our neighborhood anymore because of something bad that had happened to him there.

I wished him good luck and got his phone number. Maybe we'll get some screen-printed T-shirts someday.

I thought later that he wasn't really thanking me for the book. When you've talked to enough people experiencing homelessness, you learn how stigmatizing homelessness is. People avoid you. They don't make eye contact. They think you are either dangerous or crazy. You realize that humanity cares more about a stray dog than a destitute person. No, Buddy wasn't thanking me for the book. He was thanking me for the simple respect and decency that John and Cherie and Wendy and I had treated him with when he was on the street. Because we'd treated Buddy as just a regular person, and that was the gift that meant the most to him.

Some days are better than others.

APRIL 3, 2021

It was Quirky Day today at Printed Page. Shortly after we opened, a young guy came in and started going through some vintage political pins we have. Although the price tag read $3, he asked if they were three *cents* each. I politely informed him that we were hardly the kind of establishment that would offer anything for three cents, as we would then be 33 times lower than the Dollar Store. He left disappointed.

Then I saw a guy walking down the sidewalk swinging a saucepan. He came in and looked around a while. I warned a young woman to beware of panhandlers.

Another customer came in to buy a facsimile of a medieval book of hours. (Those are religious books that instructed people when to do what – usually to pray). He told me he is a game designer and likes medieval motifs. He spent 15 years as a medieval re-creator. He liked to help the other guys develop personal crests, and he rattled off a series of words that described the elements of a crest, then drew one for me. He presented me with the finished crest to keep. He said he had been ill lately or he would have been in earlier for the book. I believed him, because I'm pretty sure he had some medicinal leeches on the back of his neck.

APRIL 11, 2021

We had a more eclectic customer mix than usual yesterday at Printed Page.

One gentleman was decked out in cowboy attire: hat, boots, bandana, long Levi's, and a shirt so stiff with starch that it could have passed for poster board. He also had a Bowie knife sheathed sideways on his belt just so we'd know he would be there for us if we needed any string cut.

In mid-afternoon, a guy dressed in camo gear came in. He, too, had a knife, but it was in a pocket near the top of his vest – a tactical pocket, I believe they're called. I had him pegged as a Jane Austen fan, but my assumptions were dashed when he asked if we had any books on guns.

A woman brought her family in. She had been in alone a week or so ago, and wanted others to see our store. Her four-year-old son – who she said had spent the first year of his life in a hospital – delighted in Izzy's attention. Izzy gave me her best "get-him-off-of-me" look, but this is one of the jobs of a shop dog. Mom bought an Eric Carle book for the boy.

Many of our customers were young women. One filled her arms with books. I offered to put them on the counter for her, but she declined and tightened her grip. She bought Faulkner, Steinbeck and some spirituality books. People who think young people don't read books ought to spend a day in my shoes, but only if I'm not wearing them.

Toward the end of the day, a young guy asked for a copy of *The Catcher in the Rye*. That was regarded as a racy book when I was his age. I remembered that when I bought racy books from the druggist across the street from my dad's bike shop – I favored the James Bond books – he would call Dad and ask if it was OK. It always was. I gave the kid a wink as I took his money.

MAY 8, 2021

It was a slow and quiet Saturday at Printed Page until all hell broke loose. It was about 1:30 when people started flooding the store. I felt like I was a bartender at a concert during intermission, except no one was tipping me.

One woman from Aspen was looking for books on remote viewing and coming apocalypses. She told me that silver had special protective powers, then showed me a large silver bracelet she bought herself for Mother's Day. She added that the Roaring Fork River was almost an exact replica of the Nile. Maybe that's where they filmed The Ten Commandments.

A young couple wanted something for his mom. He said his mom and dad read to each other every night, and he wanted a recommendation. I thought of a sweet collec-

tion of short mystery stories titled *Until Death Do Us Part: Stories of Spousal Murder To Warm the Heart,* but instead recommended a book of poetry. And here is where that strange phenomenon reared its head again: They bought a book I had put on the shelves a mere two hours earlier. Another woman bought a book of Tennyson poetry that I had also just stocked.

As I was ringing up another couple, they started dancing to the music playing in the store: a jazz album by Ben Webster. The guy seemed miffed when I tried to cut in.

People bought books on paganism, the Civil War, physics, religion...novels by Huxley, Angelou, Faulkner... Arthur Conan Doyle, Beatrix Potter and Lewis Carroll.... A woman wanted recommendations for her book club. I suggested *Where the Crawdads Sing,* and another customer swooned with approval, sealing the sale. A man wanted some mystery recommendations for his mother. I called my partner/mystery expert John and put the customer on the phone.

And then it stopped. It was 3:30, and for the first time since I was on a corporate expense account, I was able to finish my two-hour lunch. I put Ben Webster on again, and did a little dance.

May 10, 2021

A rainy day in Denver wasn't enough to dampen the interest of the customers visiting Printed Page.

A couple from LA lingered for a long time before settling on a Gabriel Garcia Marquez novel, an anthology of horror stories, and a book about hobos, which is what the homeless were called in the early 20th century. The book triggered a memory: My dad rode the rails in his youth. During a stop in Omaha, he got some bathtub gin that caused a day's worth of blindness. As Dad told the story, the loss of sight didn't seem to alarm him. Maybe because he was in Nebraska and there isn't much to see.

A man came in asking for book about California. He was a talker. He groused about the growth in Denver since he arrived in the 70s. He said he was going to have to move because too many people had moved here since he moved here.

A young man from Arkansas bought a $5 copy of *To Kill a Mockingbird*. He paid with three $2 bills. I wished I'd had a silver dollar to give him in change.

A man named Duane brought some books to sell, calling three times along the way for directions. He had a book about the Kennedy assassination someone had filled with newspaper clippings. A few minutes later, a woman called asking if we had "any books by Garrison." Through careful probing questions, I ascertained she meant Jim Garrison, the attorney who had the conspiracy theory about the Kennedy assassination. Weird.

Two young women came in and spent a couple hours sitting on the floor sifting through books before settling on some literature. I like it when people take their time to explore and debate what to buy. As they paid and left, it occurred to me that they weren't here in the 70s, either.

MAY 22, 2021

Conclusions I leapt to during a day at Printed Page:

-If you wear a sweatshirt with "Colorado" on it, you are not from Colorado.

-If you want books about math, you aren't a good conversationalist.

-If you come in holding a silver teapot and a metal goat sculpture, you're interested in fly fishing.

-If you ask me if I've read all the books in the store, you are not a book person, and most likely will not buy a book.

-If you ask me if we have a copy of *How To Kill a Mockingbird,* I am going to direct you to the hunting section, just because.

-If you ask me where we got all these books, I am going to tell you "unlocked cars." There is a 50/50 chance you will laugh.

JUNE 3, 2021

This was a weird day at Printed Page. I didn't have any sales until late afternoon. In the meantime, we had...

...a guy who asked if we were hiring. I said we didn't have employees. He said he had to ask as a requirement of his unemployment insurance.

....two guys who made beelines to the art section and within seconds made additional beelines to the exit.

...a family from Seattle uninterested in books but highly interested in shop dog Izzy and in showing me photos and describing the behavior of their dog.

...and people asking the same tired questions: "What's the oldest book in here?" (1717) "Have you read all these books?" (No) "How long have you been here?" (Since about 10:15.)

Finally came a small rush of people who started buying. I heard one customer moaning in the back of the store. He was quite large, and I thought he was sick, but he was just looking at photos in cookbooks and having some kind of pork rapture.

JUNE 26, 2021

Some old customers visited today for the first time since Covid. That was good and bad.

An English teacher told me how happy he was to finally be able to come in again. He collects Pulitzer Prize winners along with one his students – now in a different state – and they have long phone calls to discuss the books they read together. We had a long conversation that could have been titled "Great Authors Who Were Horrible Human Beings."

Another couple also broke their quarantine. As they were getting ready to leave, the guy asked me if I would sell him a beautiful first edition of *The Great Santini* for $50 – half of what it was marked. (Comparable copies are on the bookselling sites for $350). I told him the book belonged to one of our other dealers and he'd have to ask him. I called the dealer and put the customer on. No sale. The customer was peeved, and my telling him the dealer probably paid $50 for the book didn't assuage his peevedness.

It is hard in this business when customers want to quibble over price. Bookstores are closing weekly in the face of higher rents and competition from Amazon and the like. We respect the people who sell us books and pay them fairly, and we respect the people who buy our books and we price them fairly as well. But sometimes, you need the money so bad you'll reduce a price. It makes you feel as if you've been bullied. Cheapening a book makes you feel cheapened yourself. I want to say to a customer, "How does trying to knock down prices work for you at the grocery? At the gas station?" Why pick on us?

The bad taste in my mouth eventually left, aided by new customers who were effusively complimentary about Printed Page. One customer asked if I was a Denver native. I said I was, and that I was born about six miles from the store. I added that this was the farthest I had ever traveled from my birthplace. I don't think she believed me.

Another customer bought every book we had on witchcraft, which was nice, but it is forcing me to find a new source for a curse for quibblers.

JULY 1, 2021

"Coincidence" was the word of the day at Printed Page Bookshop. A woman drove up from Alamosa to sell us some books. I hesitated to buy a couple of nice Nathaniel Hawthorne books. "I don't remember the last time anyone asked for Hawthorne," I told her, but I bought them nonetheless, in part to compensate her for her long drive.

A couple came in from Kansas. He is a special collections librarian, and she is a bookseller. They reminded me of pioneers crossing the prairie, thirsty for water, eager to tell of their travels and to ask our advice on which route to take. The guy asked if we had any – wait for it – Nathaniel Hawthorne. Well, yes, now that you ask. I showed him the books I'd just bought, but he wasn't interested. I kicked myself.

Two customers in a row bought copies of *The Art of War.* I've never seen that happen with any book.

A glassy-eyed woman wandered in. She was unsteady on her feet. I asked her if everything was ok. She just grunted and made her way around the store. As she left, I saw she was carrying an empty vodka bottle.

An enduring challenge in the used book business is finding good books. We've had a long drought, but now that's changed. On the way to look at a big private library, I got a call from a woman in Switzerland wanting to sell her father's large collection in Denver. On the way home, I got a call from a CU prof wanting to sell her collection. At lunch came a call from a guy wanting to sell his mystery collection. Suddenly, I felt as if I was drinking from a firehose that had pushed the envelope.

Earlier in the day, a friend called to see if we had a copy of *Endurance*. I didn't have one. But, at the house that was selling all the books, there was a copy. And I got it. Sometimes, that's just the way the chips crumble.

JULY 2, 2021

Fridays are usually subdued at Printed Page, particularly on holiday weekends, but this one was far from it. Three people were waiting for me to open so they could sell me books. I was sorry to tell the first two women that the books they had inherited from a grandparent were virtually worthless. A big misconception is that old books are valuable books. Usually, old books are just old books. I did buy a pretty copy of *Alice in Wonderland* more out of sympathy than necessity.

Next up was a woman with several boxes of books. She'd apparently looked up prices for the books on out-ofyourfreakingmind.com and had attached sticky notes to each one. The first book I saw was a jacketless *Gone with the Wind,* a reprint, which she had valued at $2000, which is approximately 2,000 times more than the value I'd attach.

I feel sorry for people who think they have some treasure because they found some copy on some site priced astronomically. I told her there wasn't anything I could do with her books, but I didn't tell her the prices were far from the market. Maybe someone else will tell her that. I try to limit the people I disappoint to one a day.

Toward the end of the day, a young woman came in and told me she collected vintage fairy tale books. I asked if *Alice in Wonderland* would count, and she said it would. I sold her the copy I'd bought six hours earlier. If only it were always like that.

JULY 3, 2121

When we can't find a book for a customer, we'll sometimes send an email to our booksellers to see if any might have it in their stock at home. Yesterday, we had a customer who wanted a copy of Grimm's fairy tales, and sure enough, we found one.

The customer was ecstatic when I called him with the news, but he said he couldn't get in because of his work schedule. Instead, not wanting to let the book sit around, he had his wife come in.

She had thick black makeup and lipstick to go with her knee-high leather boots and black dress. She told me the book meant a lot to her family because they had named their son Grimm. I know what you're thinking, because I was too, but the last name was not Reaper.

A young couple came in. The guy went over to our history section, started pulling books out and using them as props while he lectured the woman on World War I. This wasn't like someone sharing why they liked or didn't like a book. It was a smug guy showing off and being condescending. Even when she tried to wander off, he would find her, another book in hand, another lecture ready. From the snippets I picked up, I don't think he even knew much about World War I.

As they left the store, she perked up and seemed happy. I can't say I blamed her.

July 22, 2021

One of the best things about selling books is that I get to help customers learn things, and customers get to help me learn things. Today I was happy to tell a customer more about Ambrose Bierce, an underappreciated 19th century American writer whose disappearance remains a mystery. Conversely, a customer was able to tell me more about how humans were created by an alien race to find them gold.

And so the day went.

A guy came in and made it a point to tell me he was a professor at the Colorado School of Mines. His mother told me the same thing later. As he was filling out a form to get our newsletter, he mentioned it again.

A guy in a wife-beater undershirt came in and wandered the store. He told me he was a big book collector, which was the first clue I had that he wouldn't buy anything. He talked about all the major book fairs he'd attended, dropped the names of famous bookstores, went on about all the fine books he'd handled. When I got back from taking out the trash, he was still going on. He said he was tired of going to bookstores because he could find books cheaper online, then lamented the disappearance of so many brick-and-mortar stores, as if those two things didn't have anything to do with each other. He left without buying anything.

People visiting from Boston and Alabama both asked where they could find good Mexican food. It was curious: Yesterday, a couple from Alabama also visited. Both were apologetic about their home state. Maybe they think Coloradans dislike Alabamans, but I don't. They bought books! And I got to tell them where to get good Mexican food.

JULY 29, 2021

I met another dead man today. He exemplified something I've always believed: if you collect one thing, you collect two or three or four....

He collected books, chess sets, Legos, marbles, sports memorabilia and a houseful of other stuff. His widow told me she's spent three years getting rid of it all. Hey, did I want a chess set?

His books told of interest in Frank Lloyd Wright, ancient Egypt, Faberge eggs, and Tiffany glass, but those subjects were far outnumbered by his books about psychic powers, UFOs, alien abduction, Bigfoot, the Loch Ness monster, Atlantis, lost civilizations, mysterious places, ESP, ghosts, ghouls, and other horrors, including one book that made my blood run cold: *Introduction to Organic Chemistry.*

Other than believing that aliens speak to me through the Home and Garden Channel, I don't harbor a lot of belief in the kinds of things that interested my dead friend. But he was interested in a lot of things, and he read a lot about them, and I came away thinking that his interests made for a happy life.

August 2, 2021

We're busier than usual at Printed Page this week because of an upcoming book fair in Colorado Springs, and because August is busy anyway. But the day started slow.

A dad brought in his two small kids, planted them in our children's section, and read them several books. He left after an hour or so without buying anything. Books were scattered all over the floor. I put the books back on the shelves. It made me wonder if the libraries are still closed.

One of our booksellers has named his business Curmudgeon Books, and has labeled his section as such. Twice now people have asked me if the books in that section are about crusty, discourteous old men. "What the hell do you think they're about?" I helpfully explain.

Toward the middle of the day, things got busy, and there's only one thing that means: Someone will call wanting to sell me books, and they will want to describe each one:

"Printed Page Bookshop. How may I help you?"

"I have books to sell. I have this red book by Ch... Char....CharLess Smith...Smythe..."

"Can I call you back, ma'am? I have some customers here who need my help."

"...and here's another. It's blue. It's about history."

"That's okay. I'll call you back in a few minutes, okay?

"Here's an old book. It is in good shape except its cover is gone. What will you pay for it?"

"I'm sorry, but I have to help some customers here."

"There's some more books here in a box...."

"I have to go. A woman came in with a bear on her back!"

Later in the day, a woman bought my first edition of

Michael Connelly's *The Black Echo.* Not many books that leave the store give me regrets, but that one did. Connelly is a favorite of mine, and I had entertained thoughts of keeping the book, which was his first. But it went to a good home.

And then the phone started ringing again.

AUGUST 4, 2021

Taking a cue from the restaurant industry, we have trained our staff to ask store visitors if they'd like to start with a preface, how those first few pages are reading, whether they're still working on it, and if they saved room for some short stories.

AUGUST 10, 2021

Most of the time I go on house calls to look at books, what I see are fairly common things. Sometimes, I get excited at a collection someone has put some thought into. Sometimes, like yesterday, I get scolded for not buying more books. ("You said you liked novels. These are novels! Why won't you buy them?")

And then, sometimes, I see something that's in a class of its own. Today, I looked at some Civil War-era documents owned by the descendants of a Union officer. Among them was an envelope with some bits of dried flowers in it and a faint pencil notation: "Flowers from the casket of Abraham Lincoln."

Wow.

I met another dead man today. His name was Chris. He was a successful attorney who suffered for a long time before he died a year or so ago. A wheelchair ramp led up to the front door of the house. A mechanical lift had been installed on a stairway so he could move from one floor to the other. A hospital bed sat unmade in one bedroom.

The house was filled with boxes of his things. His widow wanted me to take stuff like socks and shaving items for the guests of the St. Francis Center. Photos of him with family, receiving awards, on exotic vacations, shaking hands with famous people, smiling with his wife – all were stacked against each other on the floor.

His widow told me the HOA was badgering her to remove the ramp, and that Chris's sons were suing her for more of his estate. She seemed overwhelmed and teared up as she talked.

Chris has a large collection of books about sports. Sports books are not necessarily my cup of tea, and what sports books I've had haven't sold easily. But so many books from so many athletes, all signed, is something you don't see often. I told her it might be a nice thing to do a catalog of his books as a way to remember Chris and celebrate his passion, but she wasn't ready. I think she may never be. Still, she wants me to come back next week, and I will.

She wants help hanging the pictures.

SEPTEMBER 13, 2021

Four more axioms I have developed about book-selling:

-If a customer asks if you have a specific book, and you have it, the chances they will buy it are only 50/50.

-If a customer sees a book and loves that book, but hesitates to buy it and comes in a day later to get it, it will already have sold.

-If a customer has an English accent, they will buy a book, and probably one you have never heard of.

-If a customer is looking for a favorite book from childhood, but can't remember the title, only that it was about kids and a lake and a friendly woodchuck, they will be disappointed that you can't find it.

SEPTEMBER 24, 2021

A woman came into Printed Page Monday, saw our Nancy Drew books, and knew she had to have them. Her grandmother had promised her a collection, but someone else got them, and she has been on a mission ever since. And now they were within reach. She talked it over with her husband that night and called me at six the next morning to ask me to hold the books. She later called the store to be sure we didn't sell the books. She called me Wednesday to tell me what time she expected to come in today, and today she did. She spent an hour or so going through the books, pausing only to call me when I was up at the counter helping another customer.

I don't know that I've ever seen someone so happy to buy books. She said she had been looking for 50 years to find the early Nancy Drews (later printings are plentiful, early ones in dust jackets are scarce). Within an hour after she left, she posted a glowing review of Printed Page on Google (no doubt from her phone). I felt good that we'd played a part in making her happy, and I can tell you that her purchase did a lot to make me happy, too.

The next customer in was wearing sheathed knives on both hips and reveled in showing off to his wife how much he knew about things as unrelated as zeppelins and Edgar Allan Poe. He bought a Poe book, even though he wished it weren't "the color of poop."

Another guy came in with his family asking if we bought art. He said he had some he really needed to sell. I noticed the left-hand side of his wife's face was bruised, and she had a black eye. She said nothing. I wondered if he'd hit her. The rest of the family, including a grandmother, acted as if nothing was wrong. I hope they were right.

A couple of friends came in with bags of clothing for the homeless guests at the St. Francis Center. Winter is coming, and the need will be great this year.

Towards the end of the day, a woman came in with a box of books to sell. And wouldn't you know it? They were Nancy Drew books.

I met another dead man today. He was a smart guy, successful in his profession and celebrated in his community. His books revealed a wide-ranging taste and curiosity: history, geology, travel, literature, biographies, photography, Western Americana, animals, mythology.... He also loved books as objects. He had a respectable collection of books about books and a lot of pricey, nicely produced books like the ones produced by the Folio Society in England. Many he left in their shrinkwrap.

I also met his wife. I believe she died before he did. She liked novels, the books of John McPhee, local mystery writers, and poetry. In a neat cursive, she penciled in the date she started and finished each book. The dates were never far apart.

They were sentimentalists. When his wife gave him a book for a birthday or Christmas or an anniversary, he kept the card she wrote with the book she gave. She did the same. As I went through the books, I read every card. They had long, thoughtful, warm messages, and painted a picture of a couple deeply devoted to each other.

I'm glad they didn't write their gift inscriptions in the books. Booksellers don't like it if people write inscriptions in books, because those diminish the value of the book, unless the person giving the book was, say, Queen Elizabeth.

I'm a sentimentalist too, but you have to draw the line somewhere.

A customer complimented us today on the quality of the pens we have on our counter at Printed Page. "I'm an architect," she said, "and when people ask me if their kid could learn enough about math or drawing to be an architect, I say: Forget it. If the kid is obsessive about pens, she'll be a good architect."

That started it. I showed her my go-to pen and she showed me hers: a nifty number she got in Tokyo that makes a smooth hairline in four different colors.

As for our store pens, we upgraded a month or so ago. We were never reduced to taping plastic spoons to our pens, but we had a motley collection featuring unreliable cheapos from banks and restaurants, and a plastic beer cup for a home. So I suggested to John that we upgrade. He bought us a dozen TOL GEL retractables, and I found us a literary-themed cup. Big improvement for a small feature of the store.

The new pens are so nice that John worries people will walk off with them. He told me he sometimes takes inventory to see if that's happening. He may regret that. Now that I'm aware of his concern, I've begun bringing in extra TOL GELs to perplex him when the inventory shows not just the dozen pens we're supposed to have, but rather 14 or 15 or, next week, 16. The week after that, I may go the other way so that he'll see 11 or nine or maybe just three.

What fun it is to have a bookstore.

I'll bet that one out of every three books someone brings into Printed Page for us to determine its value is a Bible. Two came in today. Everyone thinks old Bibles are valuable – and by "old" we're not talking about something from the 15th century, but rather something much newer. No other book has been printed as many times, so most Bibles have no monetary value.

The first guy said he wanted to give his Bible to his kid, but the kid announced he was an atheist, so if we wouldn't buy the Bible, "I'll throw it into a fire." I suggested he not do that, in part on general principles, in part because I'm a little superstitious, and also because if it got around that I was encouraging book-burning, someone would want me to run for the school board.

The next would-be Bible salesman had his in a box. It was beat to hell and, as he got it out of the box, pieces of brittle paper rained over the counter. I told him it would cost far more to repair the Bible than he could ever sell it for, but he repackaged it and left. I don't think he was a believer – in me, anyway.

A woman bought some books and had trouble signing the credit card slip. She tried repeatedly before I reached over and pressed the button on the top of the pen that pushes the business part out the other end. She gave me a dirty look. Later I tore a piece of tape off a dispenser to help her wrap a book, and she commented that I was skilled in the operation of all manner of store devices. I told her we had a rigorous training regimen.

My last customer asked if we had a copy of Munro Leaf's *Ferdinand*. We did. She told me she looked for copies at every bookstore she visits. It's a sweet story of a bull named Ferdinand who would rather smell flowers than fight in the arena. That was enough to get the book burned by the Nazis because it promoted pacifism. For her, it is a kind of North Star that makes her happy every time she reads it, and every time she gives it. She wanted me to find her an early copy – it came out in 1936 – and, after she left, I did. I look forward to calling her tomorrow with the news. That will make me happy.

November 21, 2021

As a woman was leaving Printed Page today, she said, "Bye Sweetie," and I said, "Bye," but she looked at me funny, and I realized she meant her salutation for shop dog Izzy. It was going to be that kind of day.

A book scout came in wheeling a suitcase with one of those spaces for the handle. He'd found handy for a half-smoked cigarette. He talked up what he had as something special, then opened the suitcase to show me a couple of trade paperbacks about some forgettable celebrities. I passed on the books. I think it offended him, because he let me know that he had a big Twitter presence and was followed by top media people in New York, DC, and LA. I still didn't buy his books. Lester Holt will probably hear about it.

When things got busy, I noticed a guy back in the cookbook section taking photos of recipes.

A preschool teacher came in and bought Little Golden Books for the kids in her class. I thanked her for her service.

A group of five young women lingered in the store, sitting on the floor, passing books back and forth, discussing authors, and having a good time. This is the approach of customers I most appreciate. They are thoughtful and discerning, and I value them more than some guy who doesn't know the difference between *Moby Dick* and Dick Tracy but breezes in and grabs a pretty (and expensive) leather-bound book to impress a girlfriend. The women bought books by Bronte, Fitzgerald, Agee, Zusak, and Achebe. They made my day.

December 7, 2021

The newest incarnation of one of our customers was in yesterday. He was eager to chat about his earlier lives, tragic though they were. In ancient Rome, his lover was beaten to death. In another, he himself was killed by fire. In this one, he has come back as a customer, and he bought some books, so we are going to refrain from characterizing him as a person of loon.

Celebrities are welcome visitors to Printed Page. A year or so ago, the state's poet laureate came in. Sadly, we were unable to get close to him because of his security detail.

The other day, a woman announced – quite out of the blue – that she had worn the title of Miss Birdseye Frozen Pea Queen in 1964. Naturally, I was speechless and slightly embarrassed that I hadn't recognized her. What do you say to a member of royalty? All I could come up with was, "Happy Holidays, your majesty."

The Karamazov
Letter

JANUARY 18, 2022

An attorney, whose name was something like Chesney McMichael Hedgehog II, called yesterday. He is dealing with an estate that has a library, and he wants someone to assess it. It looked to me like one of those capers involving a dysfunctional family, a suspicious death of the scion, a spooky mansion, and a blonde who likes her gin sloe and her men fast. I'm game.

JANUARY 23, 2022

The people who buy children's books at Printed Page usually aren't children. They're adult collectors who are on a quest to find all the Hardy Boys books, or first editions of Dr. Seuss, or that book they loved so much as a child about the hamster that lost its banjo. Sometimes, a parent will bring kids in and let them shop for themselves – and we have plenty of books that can fit a six-year-old's budget.

But it doesn't always work that way.

The store was packed Saturday when a man in work boots and overalls caught my attention. "My daughter has a question for you," he said. A girl about six looked up at me. "Do you have 'Peter Pan'?"

"We better," I answered, and led her and dad back to the children's section. I hoped to find several copies for them to choose from, but we had only one, and it was a fancy edition signed by the illustrator, Michael Hague. It was $80. I left it for her and dad to look at. A few minutes later, he brought the book to the counter and bought it.

I felt badly that the book wasn't cheaper, but since it was another dealer's book, I couldn't knock anything off the price. It bothered me the rest of the day.

But then I thought maybe I should think of that in a different way. Maybe this book will be special to that little girl and her dad. Maybe he'll read it to her again and again. And when she's ready, maybe she'll read it over and over, and maybe when she has a daughter, she'll read it to her, and maybe that $80 will be worth every cent and more. *Peter Pan* teaches us to believe such possibilities, doesn't it?

JANUARY 30, 2022

I met another dead man today. His name was Richard, and he had willed his house and everything in it to a friend, who has spent the last year trying to clear the place out. I don't know what killed Richard, but I suspect it was smoking. The walls were a dark yellow, with stark white squares where pictures had hung. It made me cough just to see them.

Smokers aren't good to themselves, and they aren't good to their books, either. Paper absorbs the smoke. The smell is instantly apparent – and abhorrent – and it takes special, time-consuming steps to return a book even close to normal.

But I think Richard knew this. He didn't smoke around his books. Instead, in the Spring of 1975, according to postmarks, he put them in boxes, sealed them up, shipped them to Denver, and left them for someone to find. That someone was me.

And what great books he had: first editions of Robert Heinlein, Thomas Pynchon, Charles Bukowski, George Orwell, Robert Howard, Rex Stout, Philip K. Dick, JRR Tolkien... each in remarkably good condition. Going through them made me feel like a kid in a candy store. On Christmas morning. With books coming through a fire hose.

But it wasn't so much the books I thought about as I drove away with a lot more weight in my car and a lot less in my bank account. What I thought about instead was why someone who clearly loved books so much had sequestered them for 48 years. Maybe there'll be something in those boxes to tell me more about Richard, and maybe I'll discover why he did what he did. Better to get to know him late than never.

FEBRUARY 3, 2022

We got a call from a man saying another bookseller he frequented on the West side of town referred him to us. He wanted us to find a book for him online. I said, well, yeah, we could probably do that, but why didn't the other store offer to do that for you? "They said it's not worth their time," he said. Yes, that makes sense, because our time isn't worth as much as the West side bookseller, is it?

Sometimes, not often, a bookseller will refer someone to us just because the customer is a pain, or because they want to sell worthless books, and the other bookseller wants to make us the one to tell someone that their books are worthless. But this was a new one. Anyway, I told him I'd try to find him the book, not because I sit around wondering what to do with my time, but rather because I think it's a good policy to try to help people.

A woman came in carrying an orchid. I asked her if she had ever read any of the Nero Wolfe books. Nero cultivated orchids when he wasn't solving crimes. She hadn't. How people get through life with this kind of ignorance, I don't know.

You'd think Covid might diminish traveling, but we had people at Printed Page today visiting from Texas, Washington, Wyoming, and Mars. The Texan needed something for the plane, the Washington folks wanted children's books, the Wyoming guy mused about the futility of opening a used bookstore in his small hometown, and the guy from Mars told me he had implants right above his nose that allowed him to receive audio and video from person or persons unknown, and that once, during a medical exam, the voice told him his doctor was an a-hole, and so he said that to the doctor, thus ending the exam. "If I do this," he said, putting his thumbs in his eye sockets, "and press, I see bright, white circles. And my beard only grows to here," he said, pulling down the neck of his T-shirt. He said he was looking for copy of the automotive Blue Book but instead settled on *The Confessions of Jacques Rosseau.* I was very tempted to tell him I knew where he could get a copy of the Blue Book. There's this place on the West side....

FEBRUARY 24, 2022

The first guy into Printed Page this morning brought in a box of books to sell right after smoking a joint. I know this because he smelled strongly of marijuana and couldn't figure out how to get the box open.

FEBRUARY 26, 2022

When I was putting out the OPEN sign at Printed Page this morning, I saw a young guy walking down the street looking back and forth from the phones in each of his hands before he clipped his shoulder on the bus stop sign. It jolted him, and he looked over at me, probably feeling stupid. Not that I didn't have opportunities to feel stupid, too.

This happens when someone asks if we have a book, and I go looking for it, don't find it, tell them we don't have it, and then they find it and bring it to the counter. That happened to me Thursday, and I told the customer, "Wow! You're in here 10 minutes and you know the stock better than I do. You could work here!" We had a good laugh at my expense.

But today it happened again. A guy asked about Frank Herbert books, I looked and couldn't find any, told him I was sorry, and then he goes and finds one. So, embarrassed, I made up some story about how I thought he meant Herbert Hoover. He gave me a look like he didn't believe me.

People were chatty today. They wanted to talk about mapback mysteries, banned books, the Hardy Boys, my favorite new author, Bill Bryson, and historic preservation ("I like your doorknob," one guy said. He works on preserving historic houses at a time when it seems most people devalue anything old).

Then a guy in fancy workout clothes came in, snatched a $45 book about prehistoric caves off the shelf, and said, "I'm going to do you a favor: This is a $200 book," and he slapped it down on the counter. He then told me he'd been at the bookstore down the street and alerted them that some books they had on Japanese swords were grossly underpriced, but he'd given the name of a specialist who would pay them top dollar. He went on like this for a while, then returned to the cave book: "So I did you a favor on this book, how about you do me a favor on its price?"

"Sure," I said. "How about half price – $100?"

"I'll take it," he said.

When things settled down, I looked up what other dealers are asking for the cave book. I'm pretty careful about pricing books, but I do make mistakes (see above), so I wanted to know if I'd mispriced it at $45. Several copies are available. The highest priced one was $60.

Made me feel a little less stupid.

March 1, 2022

I met another dead man today. It was one of the saddest introductions I've ever had.

George made it easy to know who he was. He wrote his name in a thick marker several times on the same page. Then he used a highlighter on passages that meant more to him, and he numbered his books on the spines and underlined the titles on his expensive leather books. All of this, of course, is anathema to book people.

Book dealers like pristine books, not only because it's in their DNA to preserve books, but also for practical reasons: You can sell books for more if they're unblemished.

But it wasn't what George did to his books that made our meeting melancholy. It was what had happened to George. His daughter told me that he had Alzheimer's. It must have been a long and difficult ordeal for her – the 25-hour day, someone once described, caring for someone with Alzheimer's – because what she wanted from me was just to get the books out. It was as if the books were all that was left of him, and she simply wanted to be done.

She went away and left me to do what I do in solitude. I finished my task, locked the house up, and drove away, thinking not of books, but hoping the same never happens to my family. Or anyone else's.

March 19, 2022

A couple came into Printed Page today. I overheard her tell him that they needed something for a shelf. He agreed, but thought they should settle on a color first, then come back for something that would be an appropriate decoration.

I feel kind of dirty selling books to someone who will use them for something they weren't intended for. It's as if you worked in a pet store, and someone came in saying they wanted a puppy because they were hungry. Would you let them buy a puppy to eat, even if it was one of those obnoxious yapper dogs with the bug-eyes? Of course not.

Later, a homeless guy who is always trying to sell us books (sometimes successfully) brought in some books I wasn't interested in. Being entrepreneurial, he then tried to sell them to some of the other folks in the store. I consider myself fairly tolerant, but having someone competing with me in my own store seemed a little much. I was about to tell him to knock it off, but I decided, what the hell? If someone wanted to buy a book I wouldn't buy, and if it helped the homeless guy, that was okay with me. Alas, no one else wanted any of his books either. I wished him well as he filled a pocket with mints from our counter, and told him to try me again sometime. At least he knows what books are for.

MARCH 26, 2022

The first guy in the door this morning came bearing helpful information. He generously shared that a book I had priced lower than any comparable copies on the market was, in fact, more than two times the amount two of his friends had paid for the same title. "Just sayin'," he said. He thought I should know this, and he said it in a tone one would use to tell a friend his fly is open. Clearly, he didn't want me to embarrass myself. He said he wanted the book, but, well, he couldn't pay a lot more than the copies his friends got because they got theirs at the correct price.

I thanked him for bringing this to my attention. "Maybe you can find a copy where your friends found theirs," I suggested. He said that there were no copies left at the prices his friends paid, and the only copies available for sale were the erroneously priced ones like mine.

This reminded me of a story a friend who worked at Barnes and Noble once told me. He had a customer who wanted to buy a copy of Madonna's *Sex,* but he hesitated at the price. "Walden Books sold these for 25% off, but they're out now." My friend said, "When we're out, our copies will be 25% off, too."

Eventually, my guy bought a book. He offered me cash for it "walking out the door," which is what people say when they don't want to pay sales tax. I told him I had to collect tax because "commit crimes" is not on my bucket list.

I should have suggested he get one of his friends to buy it.

I met another dead woman today. Louella was an accomplished artist. She read extensively on African, Caribbean, and American Black artists. Her house was furnished with African masks, fabric art, and ceramics. She had boxes upon boxes of books, mostly about Black history and art. She also had some children's books featuring children of color, which was a real bonus: The food bank we donate books to has a scarcity of children's books that feature anything other than white kids.

Louella had a large portrait of an ancestor in her bedroom. He was white. Louella's family migrated to Colorado from Oklahoma. My inference based on some of her books is that they came to Colorado during the Dust Bowl.

Anyway, her kids were born and grew up here. I was told they were very close to her and were happy she lived such a full life. I packed up some books and left in a good mood, thinking that's the way to live your life: doing things you love, learning about your past, having people think you've lived a good life, and maybe even saying, "Dan died happy. And only 103. So young."

Saturday at Printed Page provided a good opportunity to share some bookstore etiquette. A woman customer noticed another customer buying a copy of *In Cold Blood* and decided she wanted a copy too. We didn't have a second copy, so she said, out loud, "I can get one on Amazon." This is like being invited to a friend's house for dinner and saying, "Golden Corral has more selection." Do not say these kinds of things in a bookstore. Booksellers have feelings too, people.

As the day got busy, an antique dealer from across the street called. "There's a guy on the side of your building up to no good." I was mostly concerned with people in the building up to good and buying books, so I didn't check on the guy outside.

The antique dealer called again. "I don't know what he's doing there," he said. I was still busy inside. I think the antique dealer was having a slow day.

A group of young women came in and started talking babytalk loudly to Izzy. "Oh, you boo-boo sweetie baby doll girl, come let Mama scratch your little belly!" Izzy gave me one of those looks, but I didn't think there was much I could do. They left with empty hands and dog hair on their pants.

A young man came in and asked me what I thought the last line in *The Great Gatsby* meant: "So we beat on, boats against the current, borne back ceaselessly into the past." I told him I'd have to think about it, and I did. I concluded it meant that you had finished the book and needed another.

When things got quiet, I went outside to look for the guy on the side of the building. He was gone. If he did anything, he left no trace.

I could hear the fading voices of the dog baby-talkers down the street.

While I was putting out the OPEN sign at Printed Page this morning, a Black woman across the street was talking loudly to herself, pulling a suitcase, and dragging a blanket she had wrapped around one leg. It used to be that you'd just see the homeless in Denver around downtown, but those days are long past.

Almost immediately, customers began flooding in. People were looking for Dostoyevsky, Dumas, Tolkien, Barrie, Fitzgerald, and Plato. A woman visiting from New York asked if we had anything about Victorian sewers. We didn't, but it wouldn't surprise me if someone comes in tomorrow to sell their collection of Victorian sewer books. That kind of thing happens with eerie frequency.

An Italian tourist parked himself in our science section, read for a couple of hours, and then bought a book about symbols. He told me this was the first time he'd been in a bookstore since the pandemic started, and it exhilarated him. Italians!

Two people asked for copies of *Don Quixote*. We usually have one available, but not today. Did Cervantes die or something?

A young woman told me she once had Donna Tartt as a neighbor. She didn't know Tartt was a writer, just that she was a shy, quiet woman who helped with gardening, but seemed to have to go to New York often for some undisclosed reason. The young woman seemed surprised that someone of such fame would be so reclusive and unassuming, but I think that's common with authors.

They aren't recognized on the street or idolized by fans, unlike, say, a second-string linebacker for a pro football team. And maybe they know enough about the human condition to like it that way.

A customer told me he had just moved to Denver's Congress Park neighborhood. I told him Lou Blonger used to live there, and had a special garage built so he could come and go without being seen. I told him where he could find it. Blonger was the head conman in the early 20th century in Denver. His minions weren't bothered by the police so long as they just fleeced tourists, whom friendly barbers would identify by notching a V in the hair on the back of their necks. Conning tourists is one of the few traditions we carry on.

When I took down the OPEN sign at the end of the day, the homeless woman was still across the street, still dragging the blanket, still in conversation with no one but herself.

April 15, 2022

April used to be the slowest month at Printed Page, but that's changed over the years so that we now just have slow days. Today lived up to that. Customers were scarce, and the ones who came in weren't buying much. I asked one guy in his mid-20s if he'd read anything good lately, and he said, "I can't read." That's a show-stopper. I noticed he had a Special Olympics T-shirt under his jacket, so I assumed there was something more going on than willful ignorance. (He said his companion did all the reading).

A very preppy guy in his 70s, who looked like he'd just come from a meeting with the brothers at the Sig Ep house, cruised in and out in under 60 seconds.

My most enthusiastic customer was a kid who had a talent for picking out expensive books, which his mom discouraged him from buying.

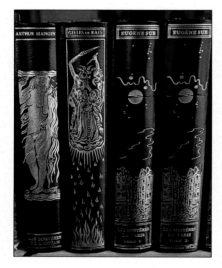

I was left to straighten books, vacuum, and dust. I was starting to get bored and feel a little sorry for myself when a woman called. She was supposed to come in later in the afternoon to show me some books she wanted to sell. "I can't get there," she said. "I'm stuck in meetings."

I was immediately transported to my former life when we would spend hours talking about the wording of mission statements, have debates about whether to use "because" or "due to," and how to capture the thoughts of an executive for a speech as if the executive actually had them.

I offered to call in a bomb threat to rescue the woman, but she said it wouldn't work – virtual meeting. I hung up, thinking my slow, boring day wasn't so bad after all.

APRIL 25, 2022

I met another dead man today. Richard spent a career with IBM in Boulder, then moved to Estes Park to enjoy retirement with his books. His son said that his mom, Richard's wife, died about ten years ago. "We thought we had his books under control, but after she died, he just kept getting more and more," the son said, as if this were some kind of disease that wouldn't go into remission.

But I didn't see it that way. I could see from the books that Richard would get interested in a subject, learn a lot about it, then jump to another subject and learn about it, too. The Romans led to medieval times that led to the Crusades that led to the Age of Exploration that led to the New World and on and on.... The books made sense to me and suggested a disciplined mind instead of an unhinged impulse.

The son went on. "Dad would lend me a book, and if I didn't return it in a few months, he'd ask for it." No, this wasn't some out-of-control spendthrift: Richard was my kind of guy. And I will take very good care of your books, my friend.

MAY 5, 2022

Among the weird days I've had at Printed Page, this one was near the top of the list.

Everyone who came in before noon wanted to sell books, not buy them. From one woman I bought a copy of *The Brothers Karamazov*. When I was cleaning it up after she left, I noticed a letter inside, dated 11/7/72 and written by the same guy who had inscribed the book. He was writing from prison. I read the letter and learned that he had a baby nearly a year old, and if the people on the parole board were forgiving, he might be out by Christmas to see the child.

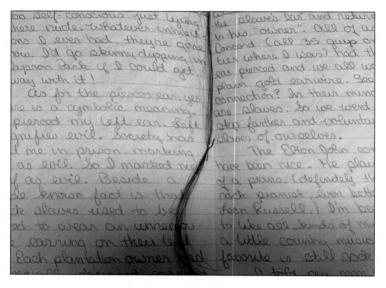

Then I got a call from a friend who handled the estate where I spent more than I ever had on a collection. It was a complicated, lengthy negotiation, made more so because the books had been willed to Michael Peterson, whom my friend told me was the subject of a new series on HBO titled "The Staircase." (Two women close to Peterson died from falls on staircases). He, too, spent time in prison.

No sooner had the call ended when a couple came in. As the woman and I chatted, the conversation turned to what people find in books. I showed her the letter I'd found, complete with a lock of the convict's hair. We agreed that the letter was pretty damn weird.

By that time, her companion had been browsing the store and found a book – among our many thousands – that he brought to the counter. It was that copy of *The Brothers Karamazov*.

I closed early.

MAY 7, 2022

I met another dead woman today. She was someone's mother, and when she died, a cousin got her books, and when the cousin died, the books ended up with a guy who promptly dumped them in his basement. "They're in here somewhere," he said, when I came out to his house.

I don't know much about the collector, but I do know collectors have different motivations. Some collect to learn, some because there are authors they love, some because a collection allows them to manage something in a world that is unmanageable. I think this woman was in the latter category, because most of the books were unread.

It took a while to dig the books out, but I was rewarded. Among her books was an unread, signed copy of *Fahrenheit 451* – a story about people who treasure books for what's in them, found in a library of a woman who treasured books simply because they are books, sold to me by a guy who thought they made his house look messy.

MAY 15, 2022

I met another dead man today. His widow had called the store. I was impressed with her sales pitch to get me to visit her house, and I sympathized with her need to be done with her husband's books so she could sell her house and move to Ft. Collins to be closer to her son.

She lived in a modest house in a rich neighborhood, the kind of place that invites developers to pester you to sell. I half expected to find a bulldozer idling in the backyard.

Brad, the husband, had worked as an engineer, but his widow said his pride was being a storyteller. He had taught classes and had published a book about his passion. The inscriptions I read in the books people had given him told me he was much admired. Brad had many friends. His modest house cloaked a rich man.

His widow had done her homework. She had all the books out and arranged as if they were part of a bookstore display. She also had a file with newspaper clippings about local booksellers. She showed me a couple of articles that were either about me, or that I'd written. One was from 11 years ago. It made me mildly uncomfortable.

We talked while I went through the books and picked out a few to buy. She seemed eager for conversation, as if she hadn't seen anyone for a while and had a lot of ground to make up. For a couple of hours, I lingered and listened, reminding myself that sometimes, the book business isn't all about books.

MAY 18, 2022

A real estate guy called me last week to tell me he was helping Bill, a 90-year-old man, clear out his house. He has to sell it, not for the reason you'd usually expect of someone that age – to move to assisted living – but rather because he is getting a divorce.

The real estate guy called again earlier this week to tell me he'd interviewed a number of used booksellers and decided that I was the one.

So I went out to Bill's this morning. We talked a bit. I told him I should have thought to bring a cup of coffee. He said that the Panera nearby had good coffee and bear claws he liked, but he was okay without.

After a while, he took me through the house, showing me all the different places he'd parked his books, which was pretty much everywhere. The house was a mess. The carpet was threadbare. The furniture hadn't seen a duster since the Bush administration. The air smelled of cigarettes, but I didn't see any sign of smoking. In several places, small bars stood ready. Scotch was Bill's preferred drink. I thought, scotch, lived to 90, make a note. Bill also had lots of guns, some of which he used to adorn end tables.

Bill and I got along well. He told me he was an early entrant into the computer programming field and had even worked at the NSA. He loved sailing, hunting, and fishing. It turns out he knew my brother's father-in-law, who owned a fishing shop. Denver is a small town. He was a good conversationalist. We chatted non-stop as I tried to extract books from piles of junk.

The real fun in my business is finding books. Bill had some good ones: fine press books from England, fishing books from the 1800s, early cocktail books, limited editions of classics of fishing and hunting.

I managed to get through a lot of the books. There were simply too many for me to consider. Bill had a pacemaker installed last week, and though eager to help, I suggested he just take it easy.

About that time, the real estate guy showed up. He said he wanted to meet me. I think he wanted to make sure I hadn't shoved Bill down the stairs and made off with his Scotch.

He told me Bill's daughter was in the process of screwing him over. I hear these kinds of stories more than I'd like. Families eating their own.

I packed up my books, estimated a value, and wrote Bill a check. As I began researching the books, I realized I would owe him some more money. I'll call him tomorrow to set up another appointment and bring him another check. I'll bring him a bear claw, too.

JUNE 2, 2022

Let me just start by saying that we value every single customer who comes into Printed Page, even if they are oddballs, eccentrics, or certifiable loons. Take today's visitors:

First up was a woman with her husband and son. I saw them on the sidewalk debating whether to come in.

DAN DANBOM | 103

I think the son dragged the other two in. Mom clearly was bored. "He likes to read," she said, gesturing toward her son and rolling her eyes, much in the same manner as if she had said, "He claims he is from a planet named Flonase." I tried to make conversation with her, hoping the kid would have a chance to find something. I asked her what she liked to read, and she answered, "Everything," which I have learned over the years means she doesn't read anything.

A guy came in and asked to use the bathroom. When he came out, he said the toilet wasn't working. Great. I'm in the bonus round now. Off I went to try to fix it. When I came out, a sign painter from next door apparently had mistaken Mr. Plumbing Trouble for a store worker and was asking when we would be in tomorrow. This mistaken identity apparently had an effect on the young man, because he asked the next people who came in if he could help them.

A man in a leopard-spots one-piece jumpsuit came in and asked if we had mythology books. I showed them to him. After a while, he asked me if I'd like him to read aloud a passage from one. I didn't answer, but I believe my expression said NO!

By this time, Mr. Plumbing Trouble had put a stack of books on the counter worth more than $400. As I said, we value every customer. But then he asked if he could use the bathroom again.

A few years ago I met Jim, an Arizonan who was building a mystery collection. Within a year or so, Jim was so bitten with books that he quit a lucrative telecom job to become a full-time bookseller. I liked Jim, and I tried to impart to him everything I knew about books and bookselling. We talked constantly. He loved his new life.

He and his brother, Reg, who lives in Ohio, once visited Colorado. I liked them a lot. Jim's bibliomania had infected Reg, and he started collecting books, too.

Maybe a year or so later, Reg called me. Had I heard from Jim? He couldn't get him to return calls or emails. He wanted me to see if Jim's online bookselling was still active. I couldn't help.

Reg called me a couple of days later. He'd called the police to check on Jim. They found him in his home, dead from a self-inflicted gunshot.

Reg somehow got through handling Jim's funeral and closing his book business.

Reg and I kept in touch. Last week, he called. The books he'd collected – many on trips with his brother – had somehow changed. Rather than a prized collection, the books had begun to haunt him. Here was one he found with Jim in Wisconsin. Here was one he'd gotten at a signing event they attended together. Here was one Jim had given him. Like that. Reg wanted to get rid of his books, and he wanted me to help him. I'll do everything I can.

Some people find comfort in collecting books. I hope Reg finds comfort in sending them away.

JULY 2, 2022

I went in early to Printed Page today. We had been busy the last two days, so I had holes to fill on my shelves. Among the books I brought in were several by Albert Camus. As so often weirdly happens, they weren't on the shelf for an hour before someone bought them. The same thing happened earlier in the week. A copy of *Burning Bright* by Steinbeck didn't survive for 20 minutes.

Early in the day, I thought I glimpsed a woman putting a book into her bag. I wasn't sure. I watched her closely after that and struck up a conversation with her. I figured if she was talking, she wouldn't be stealing. She bought some books.

A woman came into the store and announced, "I don't read books." I thought about asking her if she was lost. She left after a few minutes. I suspect she went to the car lot down the street to announce that she doesn't drive.

A guy who was in the store at the time told me he lives in a camper and travels the country, stopping at our store once a year to buy books. He thrives on the solitary nature of his life. A visit to a grocery once in a while satisfies any need he has for socializing.

He had overheard the woman who doesn't read and wanted to talk about her. To readers, people who don't read are mildly alien, not fully understandable. And there are millions of them.

I often get people in the store who say they don't have time to read, as if those of us who do are somehow skipping productive tasks, malingering as they make the world go round. Anyway, the nomad told me he is just fine not being around people, but books are another matter. He needs books. He left, headed somewhere north, with a bag of new friends to keep him company.

JULY 17, 2022

I met another dead man today. His widow called to ask me to come out to look at his "large book collection," and although I usually try to find out more about a collection before I do a house call, I have a weakness for widows and didn't do my usual screening.

The house was one of those huge ostentatious houses in the southeast suburbs with a fake stone facade and enough concrete to add ten degrees to the 95-degree day. Inside, it was dark and felt like a mausoleum. The widow told me she was moving because she couldn't manage a house that big.

I never learned the dead man's name, but I learned that he liked his books old. The books didn't suggest a field of interest, nor much discernment on behalf of the collector. Many had detached covers and damaged bindings. The "large" in "large collection" turned out to be a couple dozen books. He also collected pens, hundreds of them, and had some arranged and framed, others laid out in rows on his desk. His widow asked me if I knew of anyone who knew anything about pens. I gave her a name and phone number. He also collected stamps, and I told her of a local philatelic society that might be interested. How about postcards? I gave her another name. Collect one thing, and you'll collect two or three, I've always believed.

The books were in a stark room. The only furniture was an exercise bike. She sat on it and watched me as I looked at the books. I tried to engage her in conversation, but it was difficult. She told me nothing about her husband, almost as if now that he was out of her life, that was fine with her. I found a book that sufficed as a mercy buy. I got out my checkbook and realized I'd forgotten a pen. She looked at all the pens in the room, then said, "I have one in the kitchen. I'll get it." Strange.

July 22, 2022

About two months ago, a group of young people from the South began visiting Printed Page. They were sent by their churches through a program called Gensend, and spent a lot of their time feeding the hungry and clothing the needy along East Colfax. Printed Page became a kind of clubhouse for them. They were great fans of the store, and all of us grew fond of them. They would always end their visits asking me if I wanted them to pray for me. I never said yes. I'm not a religious person, but at the same time, I wouldn't turn down any divine intervention.

This morning, three of the group came in with thank-you notes for us. We write a lot of thank-you notes to customers, but getting one, that's unusual. It was a sweet note thanking me for my friendship, and it made my day. The rest of the day wasn't bad either.

A couple came in. They weren't in the store more than a few minutes when the guy got excited and brought a book about the cosmos to the counter. "I wrote this book!" he said, "and you have it. I'm impressed! I'll sign it." While he was doing that, his wife piled a bunch of books on the counter. It was my turn to be impressed.

About that time, a woman came into the store. She's a Facebook friend I'd never met face-to-face, and she traveled clear from California to visit our store and meet me. Later, if she had the time, she wanted to go to the wedding of her goddaughter. I think I have that priority right.

A young guy looking for Cormac McCarthy books found a couple. As we chatted, he told me that he'd nearly died while hiking and had to be airlifted to a hospital. He said he worked in technology, but the experience had him re-thinking his life.

It is a curious thing, but not unusual, that people will just open up to us. A fellow bookseller used to say this was common to bartenders, barbers, and booksellers. I like that.

It was a busy day. I sold a lot of books. I left the store in a good mood, thankful for the kind of life I get to lead and the kind of people I get to meet.

Maybe some of those prayers had been answered.

July 31, 2022

I met another dead woman today. She lived in a house in Southwest Denver that showed the signs of someone who had given up on housekeeping. A china cabinet had cardboard taped over some broken glass. The backdoor had two-by-fours across it and had been nailed shut. Oxygen bottles lined the carpet in front of a sofa. I learned later that she had Alzheimer's.

She had been a teacher at an exclusive girls's school in suburban Denver. She taught English, and from what I could infer from the books on her shelves, drama. But her passion was mysteries. She had almost no literature, but she had a houseful of mysteries, most from contemporary authors, many unsaleable. Mysteries are kind of like that, with a few exceptions.

The daughter took on the task of finding the books new homes as if it was a promise she had made to her mother. She said more than once that she was the child of an English teacher, and throwing books away was heresy. "I'm no Nazi," she said.

The books were mostly in a dark basement, where they lined the walls of half the room and filled box after box. The other half of the room was a bar decorated with Broncos memorabilia, including a fake portable television that was really a beer cooler: That was from the Dad's side of the family. The daughter said he had died from cancer she thought was caused by Agent Orange.

As devoted as Mom was to reading, Dad was to the Broncos. A stubborn man, he once took to duct-taping cans of beer to his body to smuggle them into Mile High Stadium rather than pay three times as much for stadium beer. Now, of course, game attendees submit to full-cavity searches, so even Dad's smuggling would not pass.

Yes, the daughter had her stories, and she told them non-stop. I had a feeling it was cathartic for her.

I wasn't able to buy many books from her, but I did help a bit to make sure her mom's wishes would not be ignored. The daughter gave me a nice supply of books for the library at the St. Francis Center. Some of those folks will get some pleasure from the books. The mystery of why the back door was nailed shut will have to remain a mystery.

AUGUST 12, 2022

On August 12, 2009, we opened Printed Page. I can't say it was a dream come true – no kid dreams of selling used books. Instead, Printed Page began as an indulgence masquerading as a business. My partner and I figured the only way we could make it financially was to rent space to other booksellers, and hope that we could rent enough to pay the landlord. It was a struggle.

Thirteen years, dozens of booksellers, and one partner later, Printed Page has become a point of pride. I'm not sure we're the best used bookstore in Denver, but I am sure our customers think we are. I think one reason they believe in us is that we're not indifferent to our customers. We engage them, learn about them, remember their

names, and find them books. They repay us with their business, their loyalty, and their own stories, which are often as interesting as anything you'll find on our shelves.

Along the way, I discovered the nexus between finding books in the houses of the dead, and finding things like housewares for the houses of the living. Our house has become a warehouse for people coming off homelessness. Outreach workers know all they have to do is call and Barb will provision their clients for permanent housing. Books help make that happen, and it's a path Printed Page put us on.

So now, instead of wondering if we can survive, my co-owner, John, and I – and the other booksellers at Printed Page – wonder how we can do even more and do it even better.

We didn't dream of becoming booksellers, but we're living that dream now. I thank all of our customers for making that happen.

AUGUST 21, 2022

A lot of aspects of bookselling are fun, interesting, and satisfying, but the thing that really excites booksellers is the thrill of the hunt – finding books.

Last week, John and I visited a storage locker packed with boxes of books. They had been untouched (and undusted!) for 16 years. The books had been owned by a writer who had wide-ranging interests: 18th century European literature, literary criticism, Russian novelists (all the Dostoyevsky I could eat, thank you, God!), modern fiction, detective fiction, the occult, dinosaurs, snakes, and maybe a 100 books about ghosts. We struggled to get to all the boxes, eventually making a sort of stairs out of the boxes themselves. Christmas morning pales in comparison. After two days, we still weren't able to get to all the books, but we left with hundreds – and we left exhausted, dirty, and satisfied.

SEPTEMBER 10, 2022

I read that there was a particularly large solar flare recently, which would explain the goings-on at Printed Page.

We've been subject to a flood of junk phone calls: places offering capital, credit card processing, discounted office supplies, cremation gift cards.... Of the eight calls we got yesterday, only one was from someone not on a recorded line to ensure quality.

Before we opened, I was restocking books. I hesitated to put out a copy of *The Last of the Mohicans* because we had an identical one already on the shelf, but I went ahead because there was space for it. I also put out a copy of a book on Celtic myths. As soon as we opened, a customer bought it. I told him this was eerily normal: thousands of books on the shelves, but the one that sells the fastest is the latest one I put out. "It must have some of your energy in it," he explained.

Another customer held the door open for a woman and said to her, "My mother taught me well." Later, when he bought a book, he asked for some tissue to wrap it in. "My mother taught me how to do this," he said. I thought about asking him if his mother taught him the thing about wearing clean underwear in case he was in an accident, but I didn't want to pry.

It was a busy day. I hardly had time to eat. I had to deputize a customer to watch the store while I took Izzy out back for her restroom break.

Toward the end of the day, a guy came up to the counter with two books he wanted: the copies of *The Last of the Mohicans*.

I felt particularly tired by the end of the day, but then I remembered: I'd invested my energy in that book on Celtic myths.

SEPTEMBER *20, 2022*

I had the day off from Printed Page, but I went in in the afternoon anyway because things can get busy on Saturdays, and I wanted to see if my partner, John, needed a break.

It's also nice to be able to have time away from the counter to talk to customers. When I asked one if I could help him find anything, he said he was looking for rare books about the occult because he uses them for his work as an exorcist – or a provider of "energy worker protection services," as his business card reads. He said that people often don't know what they're summoning when they use printed spirit evocations. He said that even an innocent novel might have the power to summon a spirit. I wondered how that might affect pricing.

Tony – by now we were on a first-name basis – said that he is a non-denominational exorcist, and that helps him get business. I asked him how someone would know they needed his services. He said maybe things break without reason, or there are too many coincidences that just aren't coincidences, or maybe your teenage daughter has bloody scratches appear along her rib cage. I told him of a time we saw a long, thin, black cylinder move across our living room. "It's like going into a forest," he explained, speaking of the supernatural. "Sometimes, it's just squirrels and birds, but sometimes it's worse." I thought about asking him if there were any laws, regulations, or licensing requirements for exorcists, but then I remembered: Possession is nine-tenths of the law.

We were having this, uh, spirited discussion when the phone rang. I answered it. The caller said he had a question: "Who writes used books?"

I answered, "The same people who wrote the book when it was new."

"No, I mean, like with Stephen King, who wrote his used books?"

"Stephen King."

"He writes used books?"

"Let me explain. You buy a new book by Stephen King. You read it. It is now used. Stephen King still wrote it."

"How about John Grisham?"

I took a different tack. "Let me ask you. Who makes Toyotas?"

"Toyota."

"Who makes used Toyotas?"

"How did you know I have a Camry?"

I told him I was sorry, but I could not be of help, and I hung up.

Back at the counter, a girl was buying a book on French Impressionists. It had been part of Pat Grego's stock. Pat was a bookseller who willed us her books when she died several years ago. I didn't know we had any of her books left, but I did know that within ten minutes, I'd encountered an exorcist and a person not of sound mind. And now a dead woman was selling books.

I threw some salt over my shoulder and got the hell out.

OCTOBER 8, 2022

Saturdays are usually our best day of the week at Printed Page. I always have a dollar goal in mind when I open – I was disappointed today when we closed.

Part of the reason for that was my first customer. He asked if we had any Rand-McNally atlases, so I showed him one. "I want one done before World War II," he said, so I showed him that the atlas was from 1940. "Oh, this one doesn't show the states separately. I want one that shows the states separately," he said, and I flipped to a section where it did. "I want one that shows county names," he said. I pointed out that this one did. "Well, thanks," he said, "but it's not what I was looking for."

Later in the day, a guy brought a copy of a Curious George book up to the counter. Unable to restrain myself, I said, "We have other books that might better fit your reading level." He laughed. Good thing. Barnes & Noble would probably fire me for that kind of crack.

We have some props in the store to delineate different sections. There's a doll in the children's section, a typewriter in fiction, handcuffs in crime and thrillers. Damned if someone didn't steal the handcuffs. Unlike the atlas guy, someone found what they were looking for.

NOVEMBER 6, 2022

A doctor, a lawyer, and a chef walked into a bookstore. I was tempted to say, "What is this, a joke?" but I didn't.

The doctor wanted vintage medical books, but not any ones that showed surgeries or anything bloody. She said she wasn't that kind of doctor. She bought a medical dictionary from 1853.

The chef asked if we had a copy of *Gulliver's Travels*. We had two: One was $40, the other was $20. I suggested he buy the $40 one and, channeling George Santos, told him it had more travels than the $20 copy. He bought both.

The lawyer, a self-described top negotiator, asked me if I would take $40 for a book marked $45. I told him if he could negotiate a lower monthly rent with my landlord, he could have the book for free. He paid $45.

Later, a homeless guy came in. He said he wanted to read a classic, something people would consider a basic book to know. I suggested *To Kill a Mockingbird*. But he'd already read it. How about *The Old Man and the Sea?* He thought that would be a good pick. We had a copy for $6.50. I said, "How about $3?" He agreed. He paid for it in coins. I think the best negotiator at Printed Page that day was me.

NOVEMBER 15, 2022

I met another dead woman today. I'd been summoned to her house by a relative who told me that this woman had been an English teacher, so I had high hopes of finding good books.

My caller also told me a lot of the books were old.

The greatest misconception about used books is that books have to be old to be valuable. (The next greatest misconception is that booksellers always know what they're talking about).

Anyway, I got to the house and was met by a little white terrier who parked itself at my feet and barked incessantly. The owner seemed fine with that, so we stood there for a minute or so before she finally shut the dog in another room.

While I am a card-carrying dog person, I'm not fond of yappers. When I was at Public Service Company, there was a widely circulated story of an appliance repair guy who was working on a customer's stove despite a yapper continually nipping at him. Finally, when the customer wasn't looking, the repair guy whacked the dog on the head with a screwdriver. The dog dropped dead. Panicked, the guy put the dog in his toolbox and went outside. Luck seemed to be on his side when he saw a gas crew digging a trench in front of the house, and, in a rare instance of interdepartmental cooperation, he dumped the dog in the trench and the crew covered it up. A neighbor saw this, though, and all hell broke loose.

We went down the stairs to look at the books. I think the English teacher had inherited a lot of her books. There were sets of forgotten 19th century poets and novelists, well-worn and undoubtedly well-read. Virtually none had any commercial value, and my escort, who never let me out of her sight, was clearly disappointed when I told her that. She wasn't as disappointed as I was.

We went upstairs, and the dog was ready. It sat between me and the door, yapping and doing its best to be menacing. Again, this seemed fine with the owner, whose arguments to the dog to knock it off went for naught.

I made a note to start carrying a toolbox.

NOVEMBER 23, 2022

I was at Printed Page yesterday, and so were a lot of people from out of town, here for Thanksgiving. It's my experience that if people come here to visit relatives, they are always looking for an opportunity to get away from their relatives. We benefit.

Our first customer wanted two books "...you probably don't have." They were gifts. One was *Klara and the Sun* by Kazuo Ishiguro and *When Breath Becomes Air* by Paul Kalanithi. We had both, so stunning the young woman that she not only bought both, but also three books for herself. It's better to give than to receive, yes, but that doesn't mean that receiving is completely off the table.

My daughter Alli – who drew a picture of David Foster Wallace that hangs on our walls – brought lunch: two chili-cheese hotdogs that sat in the bag getting cold while a customer lingered debating whether to spend $10 on a book. I finally couldn't take it any longer and wolfed down the delicacies, not caring how it looked or sounded. Within an hour, they had settled into my stomach and had formed what felt like a concrete basketball.

While I was in the bathroom later, I heard someone calling. It was a homeless guy who wanted me to know that he knew the guy who had busted up the bench on our porch a few days ago. He said the guy had also damaged a couple other stores on the block, but my visitor had accosted him with his fists and pummeled the excrement from the man who liked intimate relations with moms. I'm paraphrasing here. He wanted me to know that he likes to look out for the merchants on the street, and if we have any odd jobs, he'd like to do them. I thanked him and shook his hand. It was rough and calloused, and his fingers were twisted as if they'd been broken and hadn't healed right. I gave him some money.

I'm not afraid of homeless people, though there are admittedly some who are scary. I credit my experiences with the St. Francis people for that, and for getting to know some people who lived on the streets. I've come to understand that they are just like you and me – they just don't have a place to live. Thanksgiving makes me think of them more often, to count my blessings that I'm not among them, and to remember to treat them with basic human decency and respect.

NOVEMBER 25, 2022

Neil and Melissa used to come into Printed Page often until they moved to New Mexico several years ago. I'd lost track of them, but Neil called last week to ask me to put together some book suggestions for him. He called today to talk about that. I was glad he did, because I wanted to tell him something.

Before they moved, Neil and Melissa were in the store one day when another of our customers and his wife, Penny, came in. Penny was on a steep slide into Alzheimer's, but she still liked to come in to sit and look through books.

On that day, Penny noticed Melissa. Melissa is young and has young tastes that include shaving one side of her head. Penny got up, started feeling Melissa's hair, and said to her, "What happened to your hair? It's awful!" Melissa said nothing and did nothing. Penny continued: "It looks horrible! Did you have an accident or something?" She kept it up. "Why would you do that to yourself?" And Melissa just stood there, taking it in, a slight smile on her face. She thanked Penny for asking.

When I talked to Neil today, I recounted that, and Neil remembered. I told him I had never seen a greater example of decency and grace, and I wanted him to tell that to Melissa. I can forget where I left my glasses, forget computer passwords, forget to put something out to thaw for dinner. But I won't forget the time when a woman who was forgetting everything gave me something to remember.

December 1, 2022

I met another dead man today. He'd been prominent in his profession and had powerful friends. He'd also had a long, slow death several years ago that still weighed on his widow. Once capable in her own right, she has deteriorated into a life of hoarding.

Her house, in a wealthy suburb, is a mess. She seems to live out of a single stuffed chair, its cushions soiled to the color of tobacco. Daily living befuddles her. An organizer I know declined to help her get ready for a move because the widow found it impossible to decide anything.

She called me because we have mutual friends. She had boxed up all of her husband's books and wanted them gone. She was either going to have the books hauled off to the landfill, or leave it to me to do something with them. I felt like someone at an animal shelter: What you don't adopt gets killed, so you end up becoming known as the Crazy Dog Guy. I can't bear to see books thrown away (although there are exceptions), so I went there to see what I could do.

The house was sweltering. She must have had the thermostat turned up as high as it would go. Within minutes of getting there, I was sweating like a South African diamond miner. The books were stacked in boxes six-high, accessed through a narrow passageway of unopened Amazon shipments, a wheelchair, and random pieces of furniture. I spent an hour filling my car to the dome light. I told her I could come back some other time, but she was hesitant to plan anything. Her cleaning lady (cleaning lady?) was coming Wednesday. Thursday she had to go shopping. Friday is the day she takes a walk. She got agitated thinking about it, so I told her if I could help her in any way, she should just let me know. I drove home, uncharacteristically not at all curious what was in those boxes. Instead, I was thinking maybe the dead man was the lucky one here.

DECEMBER 15, 2022

At our open house last night, a woman took a sip of wine and asked, "Do you have your inventory online?" I considered her question, took a sip of beer, and said, "No."

I'm sure that not selling online diminishes our sales. Most of our fellow booksellers sell online, and it's an important part of their business. I used to sell online but I'm also sure that I don't want to do it again. When I sold online, I spent most of my time sitting at a computer, describing books in great detail and uploading them to various bookselling sites. My packaging supplier was happy to see me coming. The clerks at the post office weren't. Faceless customers were just names on address labels.

Sometimes, I'd try to contact them to try to interest them in other books I thought they might like, but that never worked out. I was in a transaction business when what I most valued was a business built on relationships. The online bookselling world was obsessed with prices. I was more interested in values. They're different.

I was also lazy. I didn't need to make a living in the used book business. What I needed was a life. So I changed my menu options.

At Printed Page, we see all our customers. We have conversations with them, share stories, and have fun kidding around. They don't scan our inventory on screens – they see it on shelves. Sometimes, they find a book they want. Sometimes, a book finds them.

Also, when you buy online, there's no wine. Have a sip yourself, and think about that.

DECEMBER 20, 2022

This was a slow day at Printed Page. No one had come in until around 11:30, when I heard a light tapping on the door. I opened it. A guy stood in the doorway holding his cell phone. In a deep Southern accent, he told me he'd had some troubles and wanted to call his mother and sister to tell them he was okay, but his phone needed a charge. Both he and the phone looked as if they'd seen better days.

I told him to come in. I plugged in his phone as he sat quietly in an easy chair, listening to our music. I gave him a bottle of water and offered my phone, but he couldn't remember any phone numbers.

He was thankful, I think: He spoke quietly and, with his accent, I had trouble making out what he was saying. He told me he was from Birmingham, Alabama. I asked him if he was a football fan – duh! – and that brought him to life. We talked about football for a while, then I asked him if he'd had anything to eat today. He said he hadn't. I gave him some money and pointed him toward a place where he could get some food. I told him by the time he got back, his phone might be charged enough to use.

About a half-hour later, I heard that tapping again. He was at the door. His phone was charged enough for him to use it. His mood seemed to brighten. He thanked me and left. I heard him say "Hi Mama" as he closed the door.

Still no customers, but at least the day wasn't a waste.

December 26, 2022

I sometimes wonder if it's me managing books, or the books managing me.

Yesterday, we went down to the St. Francis Apartments to serve coffee and donuts to make the residents' Christmas morning a little warmer. We ended up there because 13 years ago, when we opened Printed Page, I went to the editor of the local paper to ask him to suggest something we could be involved in that would help the community. It wasn't a purely unselfish motive that led me there. I thought that if I could build a relationship with the editor, we'd find a warmer reception when we approached the paper for publicity for the store.

The editor, Paul Kashmann (who would later become a Denver City Councilman), suggested East Denver FISH, one of the few Denver food banks that delivers food. I started making food deliveries for FISH, and set up some food drives in the store. Five years ago, FISH was involved in stocking food for the new St. Francis Apartments for people coming off homelessness. Barb came along with me that day. Our task was to stock food, and also to put a blanket in every apartment and a stopper in the kitchen sinks – final details before opening.

Something about seeing the homeless residents lined up in the sub-freezing cold for the apartment to open – or maybe the example of the apartments' remarkable housing director – lit a spark in Barb. First, she decided to round up 50 table lamps for the apartments. Then she decided to organize Friday coffees and Bingo games. Before I knew it, she and our friend Jan were spending hours a week working at St. Francis and were now providing all kinds of things for the residents and their new apartments. Then Denver's homeless outreach workers started calling when they were able to house someone – they knew where to go to get apartments provisioned.

Printed Page stocked a library at St. Francis, and then other St. Francis facilities. It turned out that houses where I went through dead men's libraries also had household goods. People started giving us things that we could pass on. Meanwhile, I was still involved with the food bank and got the idea to distribute kids' books with food deliveries. Last year, a second food bank asked if they could also get books. We said yes.

Yesterday – Christmas – I listened to some of the residents reminisce about their lives before St. Francis. One told of his daily routine, structured to ensure that he could get a good place in line for food handouts, and save room at a table for his friends. Another talked about the lengths she went to stay warm on the streets in winter. One talked about how much it meant to her to finally have a place for her dogs. Over a cup of hot chocolate, a resident explained to me that given the hundreds of millions of houses Santa had to visit, the only way he could do it is by time travel.

In the corner of the community room is the bookcase we stocked.

I drove home thinking how much my life has changed since we opened Printed Page, of the unexpected roads it had led to, and the people we have met along the way. And whether I'm managing books, or they're managing me, a lot of good things have happened because of them.